Collins Children's Pictorial Atlas
Collins
An imprint of HarperCollins*Publishers*
77-85 Fulham Palace Road
London
W6 8JB

© HarperCollins*Publishers* 2007
Maps © Collins Bartholomew Ltd 2007

First published 2007
ISBN 978-0-00-724783-7
Imp 001
Collins ® is a registered trademark of
HarperCollins*Publishers* Ltd

British Library Cataloguing in Publication Data
A catalogue record for this book is available from the British Library.

Printed and bound in Singapore

All mapping in this atlas is generated from Collins Bartholomew digital
databases. Collins Bartholomew, the UK's leading independent
geographical information supplier, can provide a digital, custom, and
premium mapping service to a variety of markets.
For further information:
Tel: +44 (0) 141 306 3752
e-mail: collinsbartholomew@harpercollins.co.uk
Visit our website at: www.collinsbartholomew.com

www.collins.co.uk

Collins
Children's
Pictorial Atlas

Collins

Contents

How to use the atlas

Take a journey around the world with this atlas. It is divided up into continents, regions and countries. Each map is full of small picture symbols which will introduce you to the lifestyle of people, wildlife and interesting places found in far off lands.

World maps

The introductory pages show maps of the whole world and from these you can find the regions with the most interesting features. You can find out more about these by searching through the continents and regions mapped in the rest of the atlas. At the bottom of each World page is a list of symbols used on pages within the atlas. Try to find the countries where the symbols are shown then look at the other interesting features found in that country.

Below the world map each 'Did you know? lists some fascinating facts and statistics.

Did you know?

- Only 12 people have ever walked on the moon.
- It takes 45 minutes to put on a space suit.
- A spacecraft takes 3 days to travel from earth to the moon.

World

The world is full of interesting places. Many countries have famous buildings like castles, churches and palaces and some of these are named on the map.

NORTH AMERICA

Seattle Space Needle

Statue of Liberty

Kennedy Space Center

Mexican pyramid

Pacific Ocean

SOUTH AMERICA

Did you know?

- Only 12 people have ever walked on the moon.
- It takes 45 minutes to put on a space suit.
- A spacecraft takes 3 days to travel from earth to the moon.

Statue de Jesus

Arctic

Edinburgh Castle

EUROPE

Eiffel Tower

Colosseum

Atlantic Ocean

Did you know?

- The Eiffel tower is over 300 metres (984 feet) high.
- There are 1660 steps from the foot of the tower to the top.
- More than 2½ million rivets hold the tower together.
- In summer, the tower is 15 centimetres (6 inches) taller because of the warmer weather.

Look through the maps in this atlas to find the other places shown below.
▼

Arc de Triomphe

Golden Temple, Amritsar

terracotta soldier

Dome of the Rock

Maps of each continent

How well do you know the flags of the world? Turn to the map of a continent and every flag will be shown beside its country. In addition all the statistics about the continent are listed. These include its highest mountain, longest river, biggest country and much more.

On every spread of a continent there is also a short activity which relates to the information shown on the map.

Atlanta

New Orleans

THE BAHAMAS

Nassau

Miami

Gulf of exico

Havana

CUBA

JAMAICA

BELIZE

Belmopan

TEMALA la City

HONDURAS

Tegucigalpa

ST KITTS AND NEVIS

DOMINICAN REPUBLIC

HAITI Port-au-Prince

Santo Domingo

Kingston

San Juan

PUERTO RICO (USA)

Caribbean Sea

ST LUCIA

ANTIGUA AND BARBUDA

DOMINICA

BARBADOS

GRENADA

Maps of regions and countries

Imagine you have just arrived in a new country. What will it be like? What do you want to do or see here?

The symbols placed on the countries can help you to decide. Look at the symbols in the neighbouring countries and plan a journey right across the region. There is so much to see and do.

Watch a Sumo wrestling match!
Take a train journey!

Go walking in the mountains!
See lots of animals!

Find out more from the facts placed around the maps.

It's a fact

The giant panda has lived in bamboo forests for several million years. Each year a panda can eat 5 tonnes of bamboo. There are only about 1600 left in the wild.

It's a fact

Ice hockey is one of Canada's most popular sports. It was first played in 1788 when some schoolboys tried to play the Irish game 'hurley' on ice. In Canada today there are over 500 000 players.

Try the activity found at the bottom of each map.

This will let you know just how much you have learnt from the map. All the answers are listed at the back of the atlas.

Try this!
China has many different animals. Look at the map and find

The big furry animal who loves to eat bamboo.

Many sports are played in Japan

Can you name 2 of these?

Try this!
Canada has many different animals and birds. Look at the map and find

4 types of bird
2 types of dog
3 furry wild animals

Where have you been?

You may like to see what other children think of the places they have visited or lived in. On pages 48–51 you can read some of the comments we have gathered from children. Have you been to the same places? What comment would you make about the places you have visited?

Kenya
We were in a big car and saw elephants and lions. I liked the lions but they had big teeth. It was very dusty and hot.
Katie

USA
I like Universal Studio because it has fantastic rides. I would give it a ten out of ten.
Sam

Index

You may know the name of a place you would like to visit but can't find the map it appears on. Turn to the index and find the name. The index will tell you which page in the atlas to

World

The world is full of interesting places. Many countries have famous buildings like castles, churches and palaces and some of these are named on the map.

Arctic O

NORTH AMERICA

Seattle Space Needle

Statue of Liberty

Kennedy Space Center

Mexican pyramid

Edinburgh Castle

EUROPE

Eiffel Tower

Colosseum

A F

Atlantic

Ocean

Pacific

Ocean

SOUTH AMERICA

Statue de Jesus

Did you know?

- Only 12 people have ever walked on the moon.
- It takes 45 minutes to put on a space suit.
- A spacecraft takes 3 days to travel from earth to the moon.

Did you know?

- The Eiffel tower is over 300 metres (984 feet) high.
- There are 1660 steps from the foot of the tower to the top.
- More than 2½ million rivets hold the tower together.
- In summer, the tower is 15 centimetres (6 inches) taller because of the warmer weather.

Look through the maps in this atlas to find the other places shown below.
▼

Interesting places

cean

Kremlin

ASIA

Pacific

Ocean

Sphinx

Great Wall of China

Taj Mahal

RICA

Indian

Ocean

Did you know?

- The Great Wall of China is the longest wall in the world.
- It winds up and down mountains and across fields and deserts.
- The wall is as tall as 2 double decker buses.

OCEANIA

Zulu house

Sydney Opera House

Chilean chapel

Big Ben

Berber architecture

Angkor Wat

World

Animals and birds live all over the world. Each have their favourite places to live. This may depend on the climate and vegetation of the country in which they are found.

Arctic

caribou

NORTH AMERICA

bobcat

bald eagle

gila monster

Highland cattle

puffin

EUROPE

camel

Atlantic

Ocean

pygmy hippopotamus

jaguar

Pacific

Ocean

SOUTH AMERICA

A

Did you know?

- Penguins are birds that cannot fly.
- They have waterproof feathers and are expert swimmers.
- The smallest penguin is called a Fairy Penguin.

alpaca

Did you know?

- The giraffe is the tallest animal in the world. It can grow to more than 5 metres (16 feet) tall.
- A giraffe can live without water for longer than a camel. It can run faster than a horse.
- A giraffe can clean its ears with its very long tongue.

Look through the maps in this atlas to find the other animals and birds shown below.
▼

penguins

koala bear

poison arrow frog

spiny anteater

peacock

Animals and Birds

Ocean

lynx

Siberian tiger

brown bear

Pacific

Ocean

ASIA

giraffe

giant panda

gorilla

Indian

Ocean

FRICA

zebra

Did you know?

- A panda is a type of bear. It can climb trees.
- A baby panda is smaller than a mouse. When it is born, it cannot see.
- Pandas eat for up to 16 hours every day.

OCEANIA

kangaroo

kiwi

alligator

skunk

yak

snow goose

World

Different types of food are grown and eaten all over the world.
This map of the world shows where some of our favourite foods
are grown.

NORTH
AMERICA

apples

peanuts

cranberries

hamburgers

EUROPE

cheese

pizza

dates

bananas

A F

Atlantic

Ocean

Pacific

Ocean

oranges

SOUTH

AMERICA

Did you know?

• Apples can be all shades of red,
  green or yellow.
• One apple tree can produce 400
  apples every year.
• Apples can be as small as a cherry,
  or as large as a grapefruit.

grapes

Did you know?

• A coconut can float on the water.
• Coconuts are grown in more than
  90 countries of the world.
• You can drink coconut juice.
  It is the liquid found inside
  a coconut.

Look through the maps in this atlas to find the other foods shown below.

▼

tortilla

pumpkin pie

croissants

almonds

Food and Drink

c e a n

potatoes

wheat

kebabs

A S I A

bowl of rice

Pacific

Ocean

tea

pineapples

R I C A

Indian

Ocean

coconuts

Did you know?

• Over half the people in the world eat rice every day.
• In China the word for rice is the same as the word for food.
• Rice is a type of grass. It is one of the oldest plants in the world.

seafood

O C E A N I A

grapes

kiwi fruit

spaghetti

olives

wheat

sardines

World

People play sport all over the world. Popular sports, like football, are played in almost every country. Different sports are shown on the map.

Arctic O

cricket

EUROPE

snow boarding

NORTH AMERICA

ice hockey

rugby

American football

bull fighting

football

Atlantic

Ocean

football

Pacific

Ocean

surfing

SOUTH AMERICA

A

motor racing

football

Did you know?

- There are different types of football, such as American football, Australian football and Gaelic football.
- Blind people use a ball filled with ball bearings, so that they can hear it.
- Bright orange footballs are used when it is snowy.

Did you know?

- Hockey can be played on ice, on a field or under the water.
- A hockey stick can be shaped like a J or an L.
- Hockey was played in Egypt thousands of years ago.

rugby

polo

Look through the maps in this atlas to find the other sports and activities shown below.
▼

curling

baseball

skiing

yachting

Sports and Activities

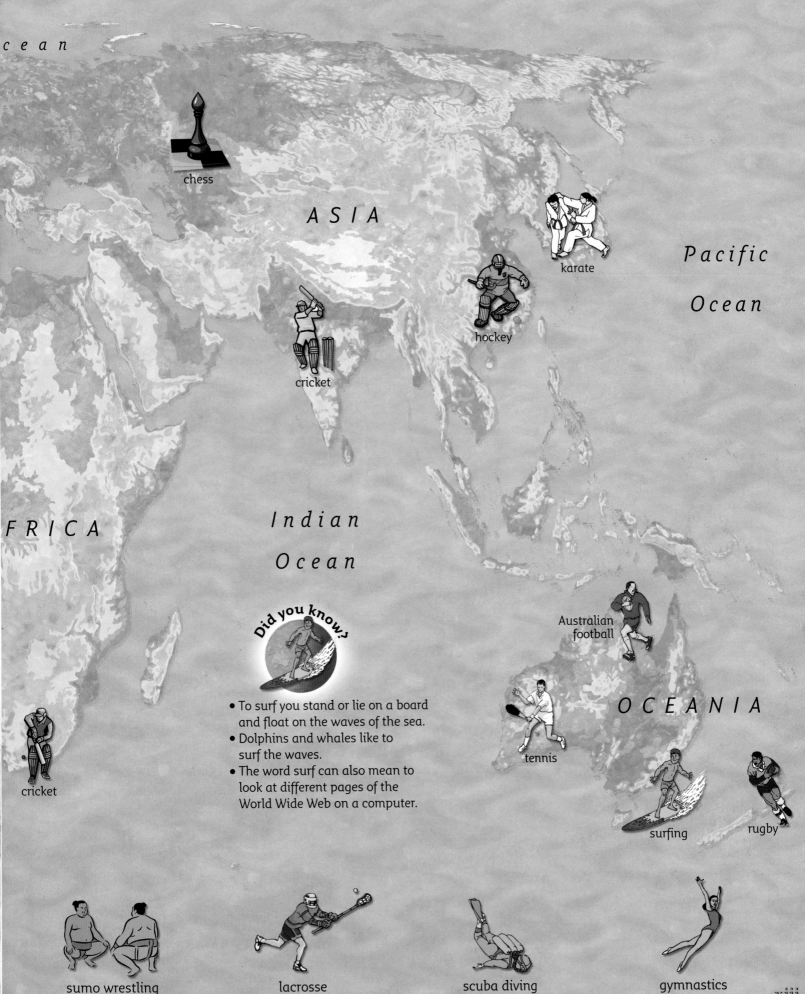

cean

ASIA

chess

cricket

hockey

karate

Pacific

Ocean

FRICA

Indian

Ocean

cricket

Did you know?

- To surf you stand or lie on a board and float on the waves of the sea.
- Dolphins and whales like to surf the waves.
- The word surf can also mean to look at different pages of the World Wide Web on a computer.

Australian football

OCEANIA

tennis

surfing

rugby

sumo wrestling

lacrosse

scuba diving

gymnastics

World

Seas and oceans cover two thirds of the earth's surface. The rest is land. The land is divided up into seven large masses of land known as continents.

Greenland

Arctic O

Mount McKinley

Rocky Mountains

NORTH
AMERICA

R. Missouri

Niagara Falls

R. Mississippi

Yosemite Falls

EUROPE

Atlas Mountains *Med*

Sahara Desert

The map shows some of the largest features on each continent.

Caribbean Sea

Atlantic Ocean

Pacific Ocean

A

Andes

Angel Falls

R. Amazon

SOUTH
AMERICA

Did you know?

- Deserts cover a third of the world's surface.
- The Sahara is the world's largest desert.
- The highest sand dunes are found in Algeria.
- The highest temperatures in the world occur in the Sahara, however the nights can be very cold.

Andes

Iguazu Falls

Aconcagua

Did you know?

- The world's highest mountain range is Himalaya.
- Mount Everest is the highest peak at 8848 metres (29 029 feet).
- It was once known as Peak 15.
- Mount Everest was formed about 60 million years ago.
- Mount Everest was named after Sir George Everest the British surveyor-general of India.

Namib Desert

A global view of each continent is shown here. ▶

North America lies between the Atlantic and Pacific Oceans.

South America stretches from the Caribbean Sea towards the South Pole.

Europe is one of the smallest continents.

Natural Features

R. Ob'

Ural Mountains

R. Volga

Caucasus

Black Sea

El'brus

Caspian Sea

terranean Sea

R. Nile

Arabian

Peninsula

FRICA

R. Congo

Kilimanjaro

Victoria Falls

Kalahari Desert

Tugela Falls

S i b e r i a

A S I A

Kunlun Shan

H i m a l a y a

R. Ganges   Mount Everest

Arabian Sea

Indian Ocean

Gobi Desert

Chang Jiang

Bay of Bengal

Pacific

Ocean

South China Sea

Borneo

Puncak Jaya   New Guinea

Great Sandy Desert

Great Victoria Desert

O C E A N I A

Did you know?

- Angel Falls, in Venezuela, is the world's highest waterfall at 979 metres (3212 feet).
- Victoria Falls, on the Zambezi river between Zambia and Zimbabwe, is the largest. It is 1.7 kilometres (1 mile) wide and 128 metres (420 feet) high.
- Niagara Falls is the most powerful falls in North America.

Africa is almost equally balanced

Asia is the

Oceania is made up of Australia

Antarctica encircles

World

Continents are divided up into many different countries. There are over 190 countries in the world. Lines are drawn on the map to show where two countries meet. These are known as international boundaries.

GREENLAND
(Denmark)

U.S.A.

C A N A D A

More detailed maps of Europe can be found on pages 22–29

UNITED STATES OF AMERICA

Paris
is the largest city in Europe

Azores
(Portugal)

TUNISIA

MOROCCO

MEXICO

THE BAHAMAS

CUBA

DOMINICAN REP.

HAITI

ALGERIA

LIBYA

WESTERN SAHARA

Mexico City
is the largest city in North America

BELIZE

JAMAICA

PUERTO RICO (USA)

MAURITANIA

MALI

NIGER

GUATEMALA

HONDURAS

CHAD

EL SALVADOR

NICARAGUA

CAPE VERDE

SENEGAL

THE GAMBIA

This map also shows the largest city in each continent.

COSTA RICA

PANAMA

VENEZUELA

TRINIDAD & TOBAGO

GUINEA-BISSAU

GUINEA

BURKINA

BENIN

TOGO

GHANA

CÔTE D'IVOIRE

NIGERIA

SIERRA LEONE

LIBERIA

CENTRAL AFRICAN REPUBLIC

GUYANA

SURINAME

FRENCH GUIANA

COLOMBIA

CAMEROON

EQUITORIAL GUINEA

Galapagos Is (Ecuador)

ECUADOR

GABON

CONGO

P E R U

B R A Z I L

ANGOLA

Did you know?

C H I L E

BOLIVIA

PARAGUAY

Sao Paulo
is the largest city in South America

NAMIBIA

Did you know?

When it is 12 noon in New York the time is
- 5 pm in London
- 3 am in Sydney
- 8 pm in Moscow
- Midnight in Bangkok
- 9 am in Los Angeles

A R G E N T I N A

URUGUAY

These countries have two capital cities.
- The Netherlands has The Hague and Amsterdam
- Malaysia has Kuala Lumpur and Putrajaya
- Bolivia has La Paz and Sucre
- South Africa has Pretoria and Cape Town
- Myanmar has Naypyidaw and Yangon

The flags of the eight largest countries in the world are shown below. Look through the rest of the atlas to find out more interesting facts about life in these countries.

Falkland Islands (UK)

South Georgia (UK)

▼ Russian Federation   Canada   China   United States of America

Countries and Cities

RUSSIAN FEDERATION

KAZAKHSTAN

MONGOLIA

GEORGIA
ARMENIA AZERBAIJAN
UZBEKISTAN
KYRGYZSTAN
TURKEY
TURKMENISTAN
TAJIKISTAN
N. KOREA
S. KOREA
JAPAN

○ **Tokyo**
is the largest city
in Asia

CYPRUS SYRIA
LEBANON
ISRAEL IRAQ
JORDAN
KUWAIT

AFGHAN-
ISTAN

PAKISTAN

CHINA

○ **Cairo**
is the largest
city in Africa

IRAN

NEPAL BHUTAN

SAUDI
BAHRAIN
QATAR
UNITED ARAB
EMIRATES
OMAN

BANGLA-
DESH

TAIWAN

EGYPT

ARABIA

INDIA

MYANMAR
(BURMA)

VIETNAM
LAOS

ERITREA YEMEN

THAILAND

PHILIPPINES

Northern
Mariana Is.
(USA)

SUDAN

DJIBOUTI

CAMBODIA

MARSHALL
ISLANDS

ETHIOPIA

SRI
LANKA

BRUNEI

PALAU

FED. STATES OF
MICRONESIA

SOMALIA

MALDIVES

MALAYSIA

UGANDA

SINGAPORE

NAURU

DEMOCRATIC
REPUBLIC
OF THE
CONGO

KENYA

RWANDA

BURUNDI

SEYCHELLES

I N D O N E S I A

PAPUA
NEW
GUINEA

SOLOMON
ISLANDS

TANZANIA

COMOROS

EAST
TIMOR

VANUATU

MALAWI

ZAMBIA

MAURITIUS

FIJI

MOZAMBIQUE

ZIMBABWE

MADAGASCAR

New
Caledonia
(France)

BOTSWANA

AUSTRALIA

SWAZILAND

LESOTHO

REP. OF
SOUTH
AFRICA

○ **Sydney**
is the largest city
in Oceania

Did you know?

The time taken to fly between
- Los Angeles and Sydney is 14½ hours
- London and Tokyo is 12½ hours
- Paris and New York is 8½ hours
- Bangkok and Perth is 6¾ hours

NEW
ZEALAND

Îles Kerguélen
(France)

Brazil	Australia	India	Argentina
8 514 879 square kilometres 3 287 613 square miles	7 692 024 square kilometres 2 969 907 square miles	3 064 989 square kilometres 1 183 364 square miles	2 766 889 square kilometres 1 068 302 square miles

North America

North America is the largest continent in the western hemisphere. It is surrounded by great oceans: the Arctic to the north, the Pacific to the west and the Atlantic to the east. The countries of North America are a mixture of the large nations of Canada, USA and Mexico in the north and the tiny Caribbean island nations in the south. It is joined to South America by the narrow strip of land known as the isthmus of Panama.

People facts
- Population: 517 000 000
- Country with most people: United States of America 298 213 000
- City with most people: Mexico City 19 013 000

Geography facts
- Area: 24 680 331 square kilometres (9 529 129 square miles)
- Largest country: Canada 9 984 670 square kilometres (3 855 103 square miles)
- Longest river: Mississippi-Missouri 5969 kilometres (3709 miles)
- Highest mountain: Mount McKinley 6194 metres (20 321 feet)
- Largest lake: Lake Superior 82 100 square kilometres (31 698 square miles)
- Largest island: Greenland 2 175 600 square kilometres (840 004 square miles)

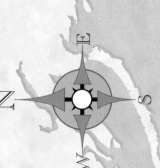

N
W — E
S

GREENLAND
(Denmark)

Nuuk

Arctic Ocean

Baffin Bay

Baffin Island

Hudson Bay

CANADA

Bering Sea

ALASKA
U.S.A.

Mount McKinley ▲

◯ Anchorage

R o c k y

Atlantic Ocean

Pacific Ocean

SOUTH AMERICA

Caribbean Sea

Gulf of Mexico

Lake Superior

R. Missouri

R. Mississippi

R o c k y   M o u n t a i n s

UNITED STATES OF AMERICA

MEXICO

Vancouver
Seattle
Calgary
Quebec
Montreal
Ottawa
Toronto
Detroit
Boston
New York
Washington D.C.
Minneapolis
Chicago
St Louis
Atlanta
Denver
Phoenix
Los Angeles
San Francisco
Dallas
Houston
New Orleans
Miami
Monterrey
Guadalajara
Mexico City
Puebla

Bermuda (UK)

THE BAHAMAS
Nassau

CUBA
Havana

Miami

HAITI
Port-au-Prince

DOMINICAN REPUBLIC
Santo Domingo

PUERTO RICO (USA)
San Juan

JAMAICA
Kingston

ANTIGUA AND BARBUDA
DOMINICA
BARBADOS

ST KITTS AND NEVIS

GRENADA

ST LUCIA

ST VINCENT AND THE GRENADINES

BELIZE
Belmopan

GUATEMALA
Guatemala City

HONDURAS
Tegucigalpa

EL SALVADOR
San Salvador

NICARAGUA
Managua

COSTA RICA
San José

PANAMA
Panama City

Did you know?

- The United States has over 250 000 rivers.
- There are over 10 000 glaciers on Baffin Island.
- The world's smallest volcano is in Puebla, Mexico.
- Belize's barrier reef at 285 kilometres (180 miles) is the longest in the western hemisphere.
- Some of the world's oldest rocks are found on the west coast of Greenland.
- 2 million caribou live in Canada.

Try this!

Unscramble these letters to find an island name.

Clue: It is the largest island in North America.

G L D E A N R E N

Answers at the back of the atlas.

Canada

Arctic Ocean

polar bear

U.S.A.
A L A S K A

Mount McKinley

R. Yukon

caribou

ice breaker ship

Arctic hare

snow geese

Arctic terns

volcanoes

walrus

brown bear

husky dog

musk ox

Gulf of Alaska

Mount Logan

wolves

R o c k y

Pacific Ocean

Arctic fox

moose

forest

lumberjack

M o u n t a i n s

killer whale

Mount Waddington

skiing

oil

ice hockey

blueberries

Vancouver

port

Calgary

bobcat

Canadian Pacific Railway

wheat growing

C A N A D A

Winnipeg

lacrosse

Lake

Canada is a huge country but it is not crowded. The far north of the country is in the Arctic region and is almost empty. Further south there are pine forests and in the west are the Rocky Mountains.

U N I T E D   S T A T E S
O F   A M E R I C A

⑤ ④ ③ ② ①

Ⓐ Ⓑ Ⓒ

4

polar bear

G r e e n l a n d
(Denmark)

seal

igloo

Inuit people

B a f f i n   I s l a n d

Inuit fishing

ptarmigan

Canadian goose

Nuuk
(Godthåb)

kayak

snowy owl

beluga whale

D   **A**

*H u d s o n
B a y*

maple leaf

beaver

Newfoundland dog

*A t l a n t i c
O c e a n*

maple syrup

lobster

timber

R. St Lawrence

curling

Superior

Quebec

apples

apples

Ottawa church

Montreal

cranberries

Ottawa

Toronto

Lake Ontario

Lake Michigan

Lake Huron

Niagara Falls

ke Erie

Did you know?
- Canada has the world's longest coastline – 202 000 kilometres (125 517 miles).
- The Arctic hare has huge feet which help it to run on top of the snow.
- Canadians consume more macaroni and cheese than any other nation on earth.

What am I?
- I grow on a tree at the end of a twig.
- I am the national emblem of Canada.
- I can be seen as a bright red symbol on my country's national flag.
- Canadians eat the syrup which is taken from the trunk of my tree.

What am I?

Try this!
Canada has many different animals and birds. Look at the map and find

4 types of bird
2 types of dog
3 furry wild animals

Answers at the back of the atlas.

It's a fact
Ice hockey is one of Canada's most popular sports. It was first played in 1788 when some schoolboys tried to play the Irish game 'hurley' on ice. In Canada today there are over 500 000 players.

United States of America

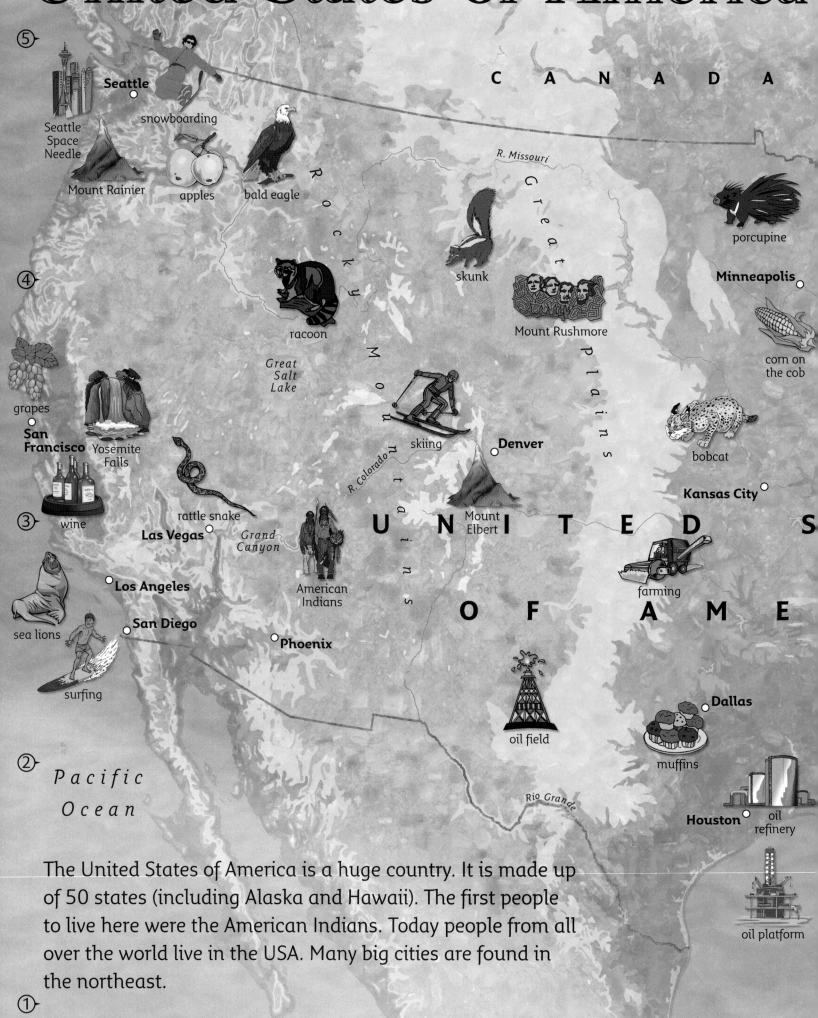

CANADA

⑤

Seattle

snowboarding

Seattle Space Needle

Mount Rainier

apples

bald eagle

R. Missouri

Rocky

Great

skunk

porcupine

Minneapolis

④

racoon

Great Salt Lake

Mount Rushmore

Plains

corn on the cob

grapes

San Francisco

Yosemite Falls

skiing

Denver

bobcat

R. Colorado

M o u n t a i n s

③

wine

rattle snake

Las Vegas

Grand Canyon

Mount Elbert

Kansas City

U N I T E D S

sea lions

Los Angeles

American Indians

O F   A M E

farming

San Diego

surfing

Phoenix

oil field

Dallas

muffins

②

Pacific Ocean

Rio Grande

Houston   oil refinery

The United States of America is a huge country. It is made up of 50 states (including Alaska and Hawaii). The first people to live here were the American Indians. Today people from all over the world live in the USA. Many big cities are found in the northeast.

oil platform

①

MEXICO

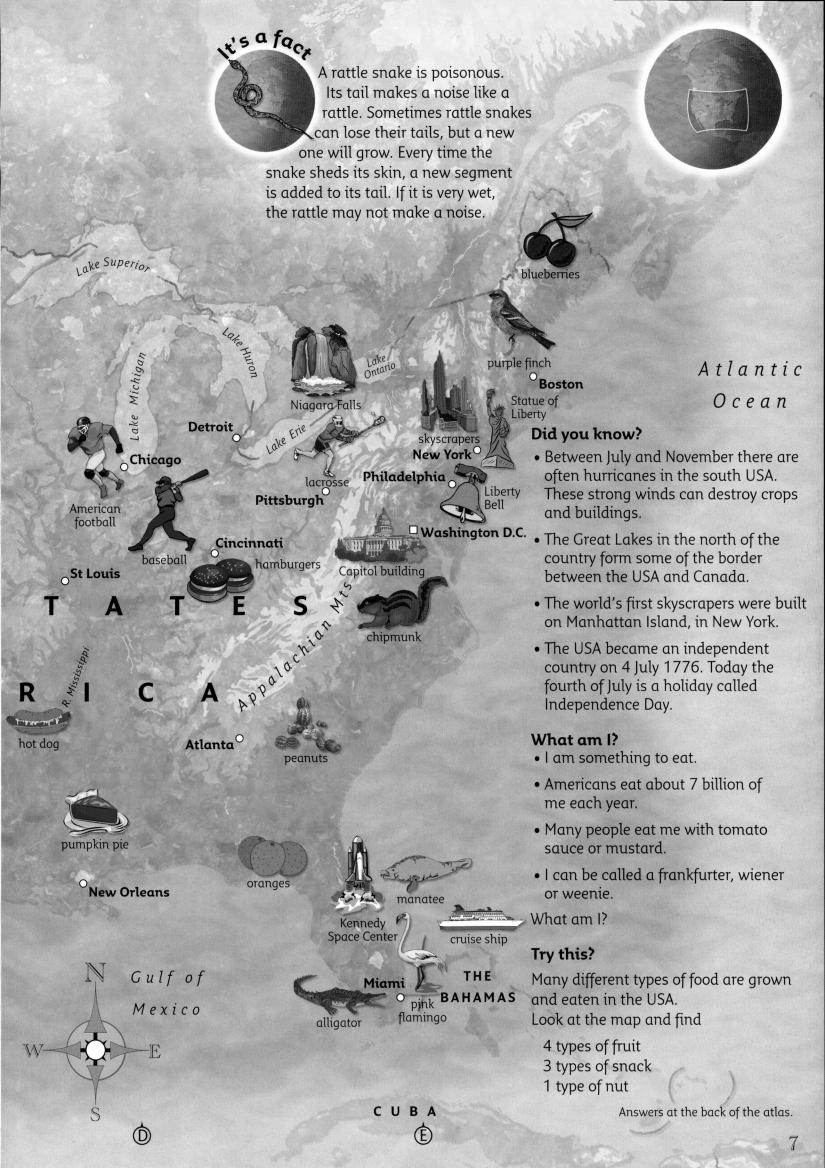

blueberries

Lake Superior

Lake Huron

Lake Michigan

Lake Ontario

Niagara Falls

purple finch

Boston

Statue of Liberty

skyscrapers

Detroit

Lake Erie

Chicago

lacrosse

New York

American football

Pittsburgh

Philadelphia

Liberty Bell

baseball

hamburgers

Cincinnati

□ **Washington D.C.**

St Louis

Capitol building

T A T E S

chipmunk

R. Mississippi

R I C A

Appalachian Mts

hot dog

Atlanta

peanuts

pumpkin pie

oranges

Kennedy Space Center

manatee

cruise ship

New Orleans

N

Gulf of Mexico

Miami

pink flamingo

THE BAHAMAS

alligator

W   E

S

D

Atlantic Ocean

Did you know?

- Between July and November there are often hurricanes in the south USA. These strong winds can destroy crops and buildings.

- The Great Lakes in the north of the country form some of the border between the USA and Canada.

- The world's first skyscrapers were built on Manhattan Island, in New York.

- The USA became an independent country on 4 July 1776. Today the fourth of July is a holiday called Independence Day.

What am I?

- I am something to eat.

- Americans eat about 7 billion of me each year.

- Many people eat me with tomato sauce or mustard.

- I can be called a frankfurter, wiener or weenie.

What am I?

Try this?

Many different types of food are grown and eaten in the USA.
Look at the map and find

4 types of fruit
3 types of snack
1 type of nut

Answers at the back of the atlas.

C U B A

E

Mexico and the Caribbean

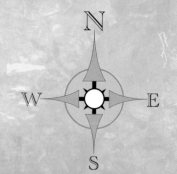

⑤ Tijuana

Ciudad Juárez

UNITED STATES

OF AMERICA

Gulf of California

Baja California

Sierra Madre

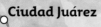
Rio Grande

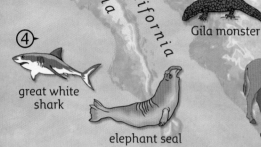
cactus

Gila monster

Gulf of Mexico

④ great white shark

elephant seal

Torreón

Tabasco sauce

Monterrey

donkey

tortilla

M E X I C O

tacos

León

football

Guadalajara

Mexico City

Toluca

Mexican hat

Puebla

Mexican temple

bull fighting

Yucatán

Mexican pyramid

BELIZE

Belmopan

sun bathing

red chilli

coral reef

GUATEMALA

Guatemala City

H O N D U

Tegucigalpa

San Salvador

EL SALVADOR

Did you know?
- The country name Panama means 'place of many fish'.
- ③ It took over 30 years to build the Panama canal.
- Around 35 species of lobster live in the Caribbean Sea.
- In Tobago, goat racing is one of the most popular sports.

What am I?
- I like to live in hot, dry places.
- I can live without rain for a long time.
- ② I do not have leaves and I am often spiny.
- I can hold lots of water.
- Sometimes I am grown as a houseplant.

What am I?

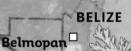
turtle

Try this!
Many different species of fish and birds are found in this region.
Look at the map and find

6 types of fish and sea animals
① 2 types of bird

P a c i f i c

O c e a n

Answers at the back of the atlas.

8   Ⓐ   Ⓑ   Ⓒ

The land between the USA and South America is known as Central America. Mexico is the largest country here. There is dry desert in northern Mexico and wet rainforest in southern Central America. The Caribbean is the area to the east, where there are hundreds of tropical islands.

Bermuda

Atlantic Ocean

cruise ship

□ **Nassau**

THE BAHAMAS

Monarch butterfly

Havana □

CUBA

cigars

sugar cane

mangoes

Cayman Is

reggae singer

Turks and Caicos Islands

limes

scuba diving

butterflies

JAMAICA **Kingston** □

rum

HAITI
Port-au-Prince □

gourds

DOMINICAN REPUBLIC
Santo Domingo □

bananas

parrot

San Juan □

PUERTO RICO

radio telescope

sea horse

cruise ship **ST KITTS AND NEVIS**

Anguilla

ANTIGUA AND BARBUDA

Montserrat
Guadeloupe

volcano **DOMINICA**

Martinique

ST LUCIA pineapples

ST VINCENT AND THE GRENADINES **BARBADOS**

GRENADA

yachting **TRINIDAD & TOBAGO**

cricket

C a r i b b e a n   *S e a*

RAS

bananas

NICARAGUA

Managua □

Lake Nicaragua

toucan

tropical fish

oil platform

monk seal

Aruba

VENEZUELA

COSTA RICA

□ **San José**

Panama Canal

Panama City □
PANAMA

coconuts

coffee

monkey

COLOMBIA

It's a fact

Sea horses are a species of fish. They live in warm tropical waters. They eat slowly, sucking up food through their long noses. Sea horses can move their eyes all around, without moving their bodies. They wrap their long, curly tails around seaweed to stay in one place.

Ⓓ   Ⓔ   Ⓕ   9

South America

⑦ South America stretches farther south from the equator than all the other continents. The longest mountain range in the world, the Andes, runs the full length of the continent. The Amazon rainforest is the largest in the world. Colourful birds and butterflies, giant snakes, jaguars, monkeys and pumas can all be found in this lush forest. People speak Portuguese in Brazil, but Spanish in other countries.

⑥

Atlantic Ocean

Pacific Ocean

Galapagos Islands
(Ecuador)

ECUADOR
Quito

COLOMBIA
Bogotá

Caracas
VENEZUELA

Port of Spain
TRINIDAD & TOBAGO

Georgetown
GUYANA

Paramaribo
SURINAME

Cayenne
FRENCH GUIANA

PERU
Lima

A n d e s

Lake Titicaca

La Paz
BOLIVIA
Sucre

A m a z o n   B a s i n
R. Amazon

BRAZIL
Brasília

Belo Horizonte

PARAGUAY

⑤

Rio de Janeiro

São Paulo

Did you know?

- La Paz is the world's highest capital city.

- Columbia was named after Christopher Columbus.

- More than 2000 different species of butterflies are found in the rainforests of South America.

- Alpacas live in the mountains of Peru, Bolivia and Chile. They come in over 22 colours and do not like being touched.

- Ecuador is the world's leading exporter of bananas.

Asunción

URUGUAY   Montevideo

Buenos Aires

ARGENTINA

CHILE

Santiago

Aconcagua ▲

s

e

Tierra del Fuego

Falkland Islands
(UK)

South Georgia
(UK)

S o u t h e r n   O c e a n

ANTARCTICA

Ⓐ   Ⓑ   Ⓒ   Ⓓ

People facts

- Population: 375 000 000

- Country with most people: Brazil 186 405 000

- City with most people: São Paulo 18 333 000

Geography facts

- Area: 17 815 420 square kilometres (6 878 572 square miles)

- Largest country: Brazil 8 514 879 square kilometres (3 287 613 square miles)

- Longest river: Amazon 6516 kilometres (4049 miles)

- Highest mountain: Aconcagua 6959 metres (22 834 feet)

- Largest lake: Lake Titicaca 8340 square kilometres (3220 square miles)

- Largest island: Tierra del Fuego 47 000 square kilometres (18 147 square miles)

Try this!

Find 2 countries beginning with the letter C.

Find 2 capital cities beginning with the letter B.

Answers at the back of the atlas.

④   ③   ②   ①

11

South America North

Most people in this area live on the low land near the coast. Ecuador is the Spanish word for equator. The equator is an imaginary line around the middle of the earth. Many unique species of animal live in the area. Potatoes, peppers and beans have been grown here for thousands of years.

Caribbean Sea

Barranquilla
Cartagena

Maracaibo
Barquisimeto

Caracas
Valencia

Port of Spain
TRINIDAD & TOBAGO

oil refineries

R. Orinoco

oil wells

④

PANAMA

Bucaramanga

iguana

VENEZUELA

GUYANA

Medellín

puma

jaguar

Angel Falls

poison arrow frog

coffee

Bogotá

emeralds

Guiana

H i

③

Cali

COLOMBIA

sloth

R. Negro

Quito

Mount Cotopaxi

coffee

butterflies

Manaus

manta ray

ECUADOR

tapir

Guayaquil

football

capybara

Amazon Basin

②

condor

R. Madeira

anaconda

panpipes

monkeys

B

Pacific Ocean

llama

Andes

PERU

deforestation

①

Lima

rubber

12

Ⓐ

Ⓑ

Ⓒ

N
W · E
S

It's a fact

Andean panpipes are musical instruments made from pipes strapped together. The pipes are made from a reed called 'songo'. Songo grows on the banks of Lake Titicaca. Andean panpipes are also called zampoñas.

Did you know?

- The River Amazon carries more water than the rivers Nile, Chang Jiang and Mississippi combined.

- The Amazon is the largest rainforest in the world. About half of the world's plants, animals and insects are found there.

- The world's highest railway station, La Galera, is in Peru.

What am I?

- I live in the mountains and can reach more than 50 years of age.

- I can glide through the air for very long distances.

- Sometimes I eat so much that I can't get off the ground to fly.

- I am one of the world's largest vultures.

What am I?

Try this!

Look at the map and find

2 precious stones
1 deadly snake

Answers at the back of the atlas.

Georgetown

Paramaribo

rocket launch

Cayenne

SURINAME   FRENCH GUIANA

g h l a n d s

cayenne peppers

Atlantic Ocean

R. Amazon

Belém

Fortaleza

toucan

armadillo

sugar cane

Natal

surfing

R A Z I L

Recife

R. São Francisco

porcupines

R. Tocantins

Maceió

parrot

B r a z i l i a n

H i g h l a n d s

diamonds

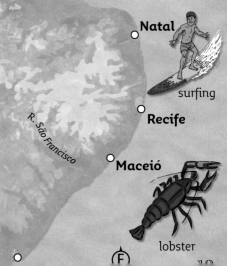

lobster

South America South

Running down the west coast of this area is the driest place on earth, the Atacama Desert. The southern tip of South America is very cold and there are icebergs in the sea. Many people in Paraguay are descended from the Indians who lived in South America before people from Europe arrived.

N
W — E
S

Did you know?

- Chile is 10 times longer than it is wide.
- The sea around Cape Horn, south of Chile, is very rough. Many ships have been wrecked there.

P E R U

B O L I V I A

B R A Z I L

Brazilian

Planalto do Mato Grosso

Highlands

PARAGUAY

A
R
G
E
N
T
L

Gran Chaco

Atacama Desert

Lake Titicaca

alpaca

potatoes

skiing

La Paz

man in poncho

Chilean stag beetle

pelican

chinchilla

Argentinian church

R. Salado

R. Paraná

sheep

R. Paraguay

football

Asunción

anteater

Santa Cruz

Sucre

Brasília

Goiânia

footballer

coffee growing

R. Paraná

Iguaçu Falls

oranges

Curitiba

Porto Alegre

Campinas

São Paulo

Santos

carnivals

Statue de Jesus

Belo Horizonte

Rio de Janeiro

beaches

- Most people in this region speak Spanish.
- Millions of sheep and cattle are farmed on the flat grassy plains known as the pampas. They are looked after by Gauchos, or cowboys.
- Almost all of Paraguay's electricity comes from hydroelectric power.
- Uruguay has won several Olympic medals for football.

What am I?
- I live in the sea.
- I am black and white and have a large fin.
- I am very sociable and have a good memory.
- I am noisy. I make lots of clicks and whistles.
- I have been around for millions of years.
- I can be called Orca.

What am I?

Try this!

Look at the map and find 2 types of fish

Many sports are played in South America Can you name 3 of these?

Answers at the back of the atlas.

It's a fact

Anteaters eat ants and termites. They have a long, sticky tongue and no teeth. Their front claws are strong and sharp. The babies ride on their mother's back.

Africa

Africa is the second largest continent. It is 3 times the area of Europe.
From the Mediterranean Sea in the north, Africa stretches approximately
8000 kilometres (4971 miles) to its most southerly point, Cape Agulhas.
Most of northern Africa lies in and around the Sahara desert, while large
areas of central Africa are covered in dense tropical rainforest.

People facts

- Population: 909 000 000
- Country with most people:
  Nigeria 131 530 000
- City with most people:
  Cairo 11 146 000

Geography facts

- Area: 30 343 578 square kilometres
  (11 715 721 square miles)
- Largest country: Sudan
  2 505 813 square kilometres
  (967 500 square miles)
- Longest river: Nile
  6695 kilometres (4160 miles)
- Highest mountain: Kilimanjaro
  5892 metres (19 331 feet)
- Largest lake: Lake Victoria
  68 800 square kilometres
  (26 563 square miles)
- Largest island: Madagascar
  587 040 square kilometres
  (226 657 square miles)

EUROPE

ASIA

Mediterranean Sea

Red Sea

Atlas Mountains

S a h a r a

R. Nile

Ethiopian Highlands

Azores
(Portugal)

Madeira
(Portugal)

Canary Is
(Spain)

CAPE VERDE
Praia

Dakar
SENEGAL
Banjul
THE GAMBIA
GUINEA-BISSAU
Bissau
GUINEA
Conakry
Freetown
SIERRA LEONE
Monrovia
LIBERIA

Nouakchott
MAURITANIA

WESTERN SAHARA
Laayoune

Rabat
MOROCCO

Algiers
ALGERIA

Tunis
TUNISIA

Tripoli
LIBYA

Cairo
EGYPT

Khartoum
SUDAN

Asmara
ERITREA

Djibouti
DJIBOUTI

Addis Ababa
ETHIOPIA

SOMALIA

MALI
Bamako

Niamey
NIGER

Ouagadougou
BURKINA

Abuja
NIGERIA

Ndjamena
CHAD

CENTRAL AFRICAN REPUBLIC
Bangui

Yamoussoukro
CÔTE D'IVOIRE

Accra
GHANA
Lomé
Porto-Novo
BENIN

Malabo
Yaoundé
CAMEROON

⑦

⑥

⑤

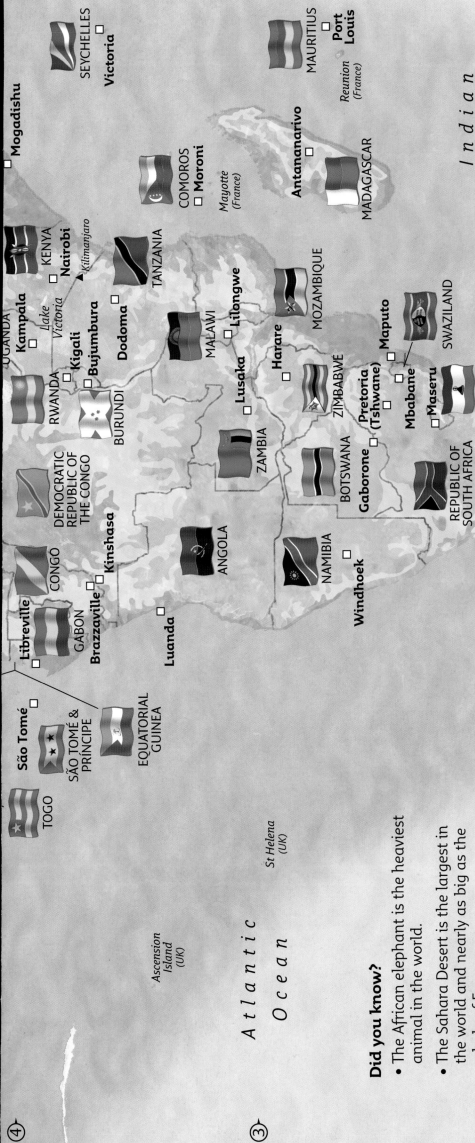

SEYCHELLES
Victoria

■ **Mogadishu**

MAURITIUS
Port Louis

Reunion (France)

COMOROS **Moroni**
■

Mayotte (France)

Antananarivo
■

MADAGASCAR

I n d i a n

O c e a n

UGANDA
Kampala
■

KENYA
Nairobi ■
▲ *Kilimanjaro*

L lake Victoria

RWANDA
Kigali ■
Bujumbura ■
BURUNDI

TANZANIA
Dodoma ■

MALAWI
Lilongwe ■

Lusaka ■

Harare ■

MOZAMBIQUE

Maputo ■

ZIMBABWE
SWAZILAND

Pretoria (Tshwane) ■
Mbabane ■
Maseru ■
LESOTHO

ZAMBIA

BOTSWANA
Gaborone ■

REPUBLIC OF
SOUTH AFRICA

Cape Agulhas

DEMOCRATIC
REPUBLIC OF
THE CONGO
Kinshasa ■

NAMIBIA
Windhoek ■

Cape Town

CONGO
Brazzaville ■

GABON
Libreville ■

ANGOLA
Luanda ■

St Helena (UK)

São Tomé ■
SÃO TOMÉ & PRÍNCIPE

EQUATORIAL GUINEA

TOGO

Ascension Island (UK)

Atlantic

Ocean

Did you know?

• The African elephant is the heaviest animal in the world.

• The Sahara Desert is the largest in the world and nearly as big as the whole of Europe.

• Mount Kenya is on the equator, but its peak is always covered in snow.

• About 400 languages are spoken in Nigeria.

• The Goliath beetle found near the equator in Africa is one of the largest insects in the world.

• In the rainforests of central Africa, it rains almost every day.

• The sea around the Cape of Good Hope is rough and dangerous. Gale force winds blow there most of the time.

Try this!

Unscramble these letters to find the country.

Clue: It is surrounded by sea.

CARDAMSAGA

Answers at the back of the atlas.

N
E
S
W

Ⓐ Ⓑ Ⓒ Ⓓ

① ② ③ ④

17

Northern Africa

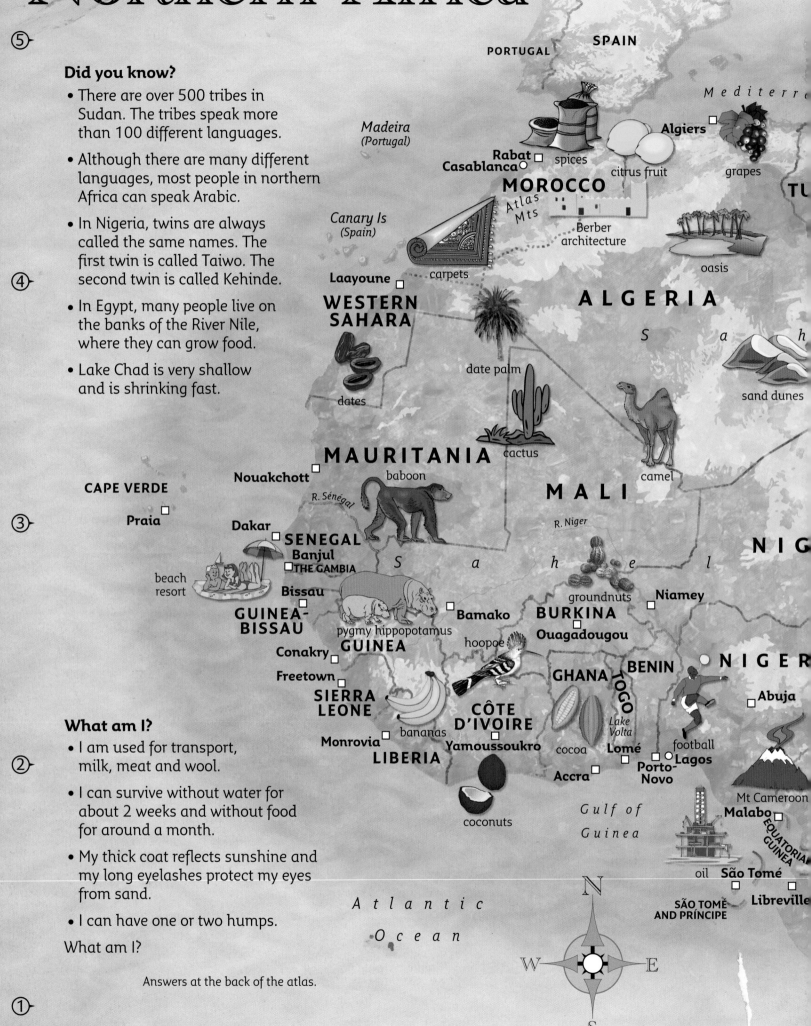

⑤

Did you know?

- There are over 500 tribes in Sudan. The tribes speak more than 100 different languages.

- Although there are many different languages, most people in northern Africa can speak Arabic.

- In Nigeria, twins are always called the same names. The first twin is called Taiwo. The second twin is called Kehinde.

④

- In Egypt, many people live on the banks of the River Nile, where they can grow food.

- Lake Chad is very shallow and is shrinking fast.

What am I?

- I am used for transport, milk, meat and wool.

②

- I can survive without water for about 2 weeks and without food for around a month.

- My thick coat reflects sunshine and my long eyelashes protect my eyes from sand.

- I can have one or two humps.

What am I?

Answers at the back of the atlas.

①

PORTUGAL
SPAIN

Mediterre

Madeira
(Portugal)

Algiers

spices

Rabat
Casablanca

citrus fruit

grapes

MOROCCO

Atlas Mts

Berber architecture

TU

oasis

Canary Is
(Spain)

carpets

Laayoune

WESTERN SAHARA

ALGERIA

S   a   h

date palm

dates

cactus

sand dunes

camel

MAURITANIA

baboon

Nouakchott

CAPE VERDE

R. Sénégal

M A L I

③

Praia

Dakar

SENEGAL

Banjul
THE GAMBIA

R. Niger

N I G

beach resort

Bissau

S   a   h   e   l

groundnuts

Niamey

GUINEA-BISSAU

pygmy hippopotamus

Bamako

BURKINA

Conakry

GUINEA

hoopoe

Ouagadougou

Freetown

GHANA

TOGO

BENIN

N I G E R

SIERRA LEONE

CÔTE D'IVOIRE

Lake Volta

Abuja

Monrovia

bananas

Yamoussoukro

cocoa

Lomé

football

Lagos

LIBERIA

Accra

Porto-Novo

Mt Cameroon

coconuts

Gulf of Guinea

Malabo

oil

São Tomé

EQUATORIAL GUINEA

Atlantic Ocean

SÃO TOMÉ AND PRÍNCIPE

Libreville

N

W   E

S

18

Ⓐ   Ⓑ   Ⓒ

Africa is connected to the continent of Asia at the narrow Sinai peninsula, north of the Red Sea. It is separated narrowly from Europe by the Strait of Gibraltar. Much of northern Africa is dry desert: the Sahara Desert and the Sahel region.

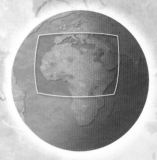

Try this?

Many different animals and birds are found in this region.
Look at the map and find

3 types of animal with furry or woolly coats
2 types of animal with hard shells
3 types of bird

Answers at the back of the atlas.

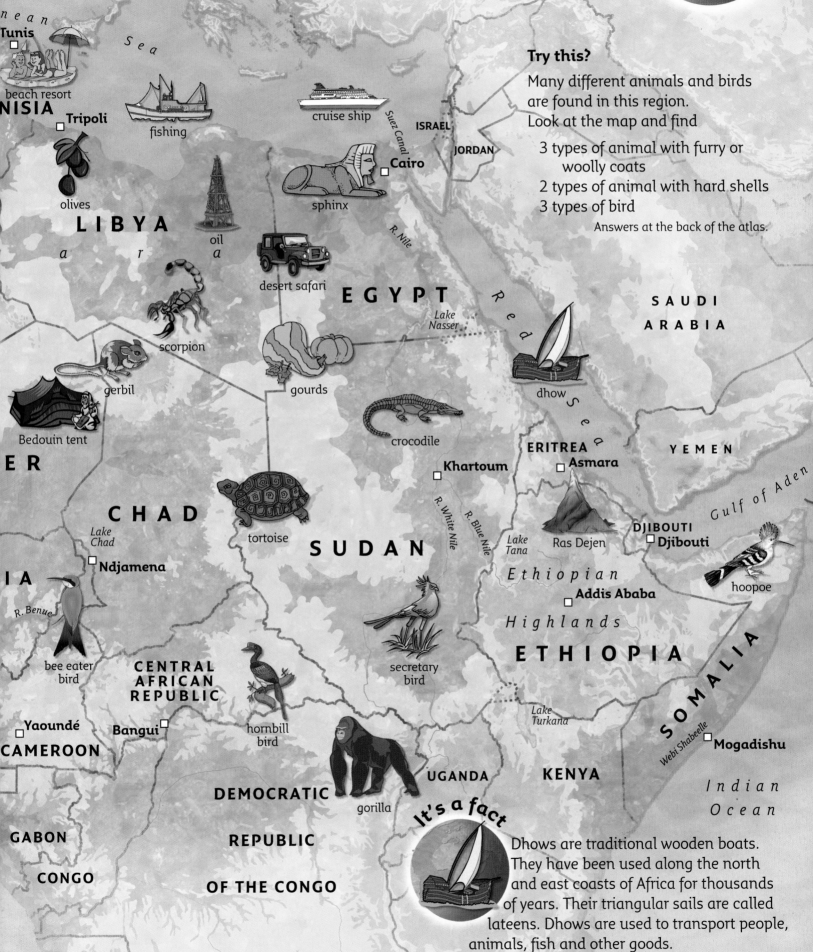

nean Sea

Tunis

beach resort

NISIA

Tripoli

fishing

cruise ship

Suez Canal

ISRAEL

JORDAN

Cairo

olives

sphinx

LIBYA

oil

a r a

desert safari

EGYPT

Lake Nasser

R. Nile

SAUDI ARABIA

Red Sea

scorpion

gerbil

gourds

dhow

Bedouin tent

crocodile

ERITREA

Asmara

YEMEN

ER

Khartoum

Gulf of Aden

DJIBOUTI

Djibouti

CHAD

Lake Chad

tortoise

SUDAN

R. White Nile

R. Blue Nile

Lake Tana

Ras Dejen

hoopoe

Ndjamena

IA

R. Benue

Ethiopian

Addis Ababa

Highlands

bee eater bird

CENTRAL AFRICAN REPUBLIC

secretary bird

ETHIOPIA

Lake Turkana

SOMALIA

Yaoundé

Bangui

hornbill bird

CAMEROON

gorilla

UGANDA

KENYA

Webi Shabeelle

Mogadishu

DEMOCRATIC

Indian Ocean

GABON

REPUBLIC

It's a fact

CONGO

OF THE CONGO

Dhows are traditional wooden boats. They have been used along the north and east coasts of Africa for thousands of years. Their triangular sails are called lateens. Dhows are used to transport people, animals, fish and other goods.

ANGOLA

D

E

TANZANIA

F

Southern Africa

At the centre of southern Africa is the huge rainforest of the River Congo and the Congo Basin. The Great Rift Valley is surrounded by some of the highest mountains in Africa. In the southwest are the Kalahari and Namib deserts.

N
W · E
S

ERITREA

DJIBOUTI

SOMALIA

Mogadishu

ETHIOPIA

Ethiopian Highlands

SUDAN

secretary bird

KENYA

Lake Turkana

coffee beans

elephants

lion

beaches

Dar es Salaam

cloves

Nairobi

Kilimanjaro

Lake Victoria

Dodoma

TANZANIA

leopard

Great Rift Valley

chameleon

Lake Nyasa

MALAWI

UGANDA

Kampala

gorilla

RWANDA Kigali

Bujumbura

BURUNDI

Lake Tanganyika

cheetah

Lubumbashi

Lilongwe

Moroni

COMOROS

MAYOTTE

Indian Ocean

CENTRAL AFRICAN REPUBLIC

hornbill bird

Bangui

DEMOCRATIC

R. Congo

REPUBLIC

OF

THE

CONGO

crocodiles

Congo Basin

deforestation

elephants

zebra

NIGERIA

CAMEROON

Yaoundé

Malabo

EQUATORIAL GUINEA

Libreville

GABON

São Tomé

SÃO TOMÉ AND PRÍNCIPE

chimpanzee

C O N G O

Brazzaville

Kinshasa

ANGOLA

Luanda

ANGOLA

Bie Plateau

oil rig

flying fish

giraffe

elephants

20

What am I?

- I am found on the coast and in deserts.
- I can be made from worn down stone and shell.
- I move in the wind and get very hot in the sun.
- I can be different shapes: ridges, crescents and crests like waves.
- I can fall downhill in an avalanche, like snow.
- I am made from sand.

What am I?

Try this?

There are lots of different fruits and plants in this region. Look at the map and find

2 types of fruit
1 type of spice.

Did you know?

- Madagascar is the only place in the world where lemurs live.
- A lemur is a type of monkey with a long tail.
- Nelson Mandela became the first black president of South Africa in 1994.
- European languages such as French, Portuguese and English are widely spoken in southern Africa.
- Diamonds and gold are mined in southern Africa.

It's a fact

Gorillas are the largest type of monkey in the world. They live on the ground in the forests of Africa. Gorillas are a close relative to humans. They eat fruits, leaves and insects. Gorillas are in danger of becoming extinct.

Answers at the back of the atlas.

21

Europe

The land area of Europe covers just over 2% of the world. It is the second smallest continent and extends far north into the Arctic Ocean and south to the Mediterranean Sea. In the north the winters are long and cold. In the south the weather is much warmer. Europe has over 40 countries and a wide variety of cultures, languages and religions.

People facts
- Population: 586 000 000 (excluding Russian Federation)
- Country with most people: Germany 82 689 000
- City with most people: Paris 9 854 000

Geography facts
- Area: 9 908 599 square kilometres (3 825 731 square miles)
- Largest country: Ukraine 603 700 square kilometres (233 090 square miles) (excluding Russian Federation)
- Longest river: Volga 3688 kilometres (2291 miles)
- Highest mountain: El'brus 5642 metres (18 510 feet)
- Largest lake: Caspian Sea 371 000 square kilometres (143 243 square miles)
- Largest island: Great Britain 218 476 square kilometres (84 354 square miles)

Try this!
How many flags are black, red and yellow?

Which flag has 5 blue stripes?

Which country uses this flag?

Answers at the back of the atlas.

ICELAND
□ Reykjavík

Faroe Islands (Denmark)

UNITED KINGDOM

Dublin
□

Great Britain

IRELAND

London □

NETHERLANDS
Amsterdam
The □ □
Hague

Brussels □

BELGIUM

Paris □

LUXEMBOURG

Bern

SWITZERLAND

Atlantic Ocean

FRANCE

ANDORRA

MONACO

PORTUGAL

□ **Madrid**

○ **Barcelona**

Lisbon □

SPAIN

Gibraltar (UK)

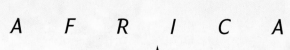
A F R I C A

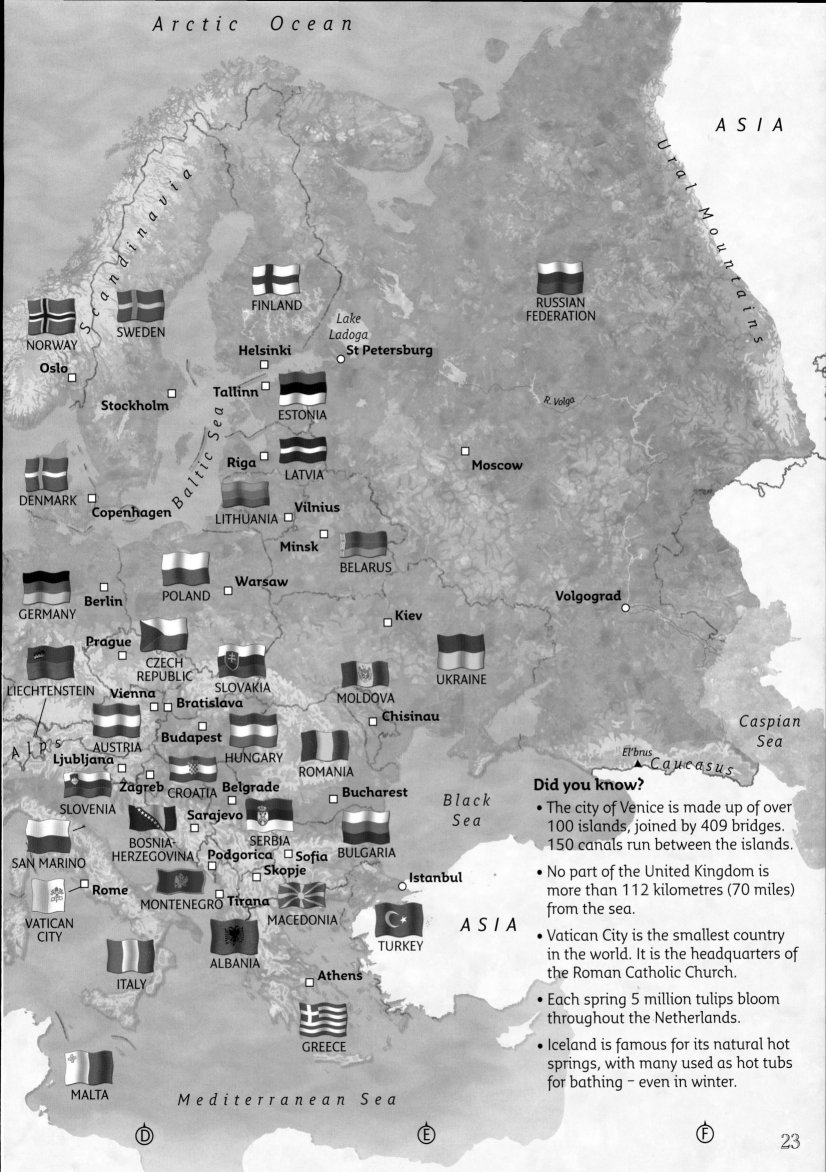

Arctic Ocean

ASIA

Scandinavia

Ural Mountains

FINLAND

Lake Ladoga

RUSSIAN FEDERATION

NORWAY

SWEDEN

Helsinki

St Petersburg

Oslo

Tallinn

R. Volga

Stockholm

ESTONIA

Baltic Sea

Riga

LATVIA

Moscow

DENMARK

Vilnius

Copenhagen

LITHUANIA

Minsk

BELARUS

Volgograd

Berlin

Warsaw

GERMANY

POLAND

Kiev

Prague

UKRAINE

CZECH REPUBLIC

SLOVAKIA

LIECHTENSTEIN

Vienna

Bratislava

MOLDOVA

Caspian Sea

Chisinau

Alps

AUSTRIA

Budapest

El'brus

Caucasus

Ljubljana

HUNGARY

Zagreb

ROMANIA

SLOVENIA

CROATIA

Belgrade

Bucharest

Black Sea

Did you know?

SAN MARINO

Sarajevo

BOSNIA-HERZEGOVINA

SERBIA

Podgorica

Sofia

BULGARIA

- The city of Venice is made up of over 100 islands, joined by 409 bridges. 150 canals run between the islands.

Rome

Skopje

VATICAN CITY

MONTENEGRO

Tirana

Istanbul

- No part of the United Kingdom is more than 112 kilometres (70 miles) from the sea.

MACEDONIA

ASIA

TURKEY

- Vatican City is the smallest country in the world. It is the headquarters of the Roman Catholic Church.

ITALY

ALBANIA

Athens

- Each spring 5 million tulips bloom throughout the Netherlands.

GREECE

- Iceland is famous for its natural hot springs, with many used as hot tubs for bathing – even in winter.

MALTA

Mediterranean Sea

D

E

F

23

⑦

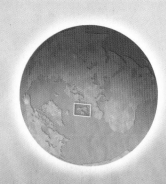

United Kingdom and Ireland

The United Kingdom is made up of 4 nations: England, Wales, Scotland and Northern Ireland. Its capital and largest city is London. Great Britain is the largest island in Europe and is separated from mainland Europe by only 35 kilometres (21 miles) at the Strait of Dover. Ireland, whose capital is Dublin, is a separate country from Northern Ireland.

Did you know?

- More than 6000 islands make up the United Kingdom and Ireland.
- Some areas of Ireland have more wet days than dry days.
- The city of Edinburgh is built on an extinct volcano.
- More than 300 different languages are spoken in London.
- The Welsh language is spoken and written in Wales.
- Many tourists come to these islands to visit the castles, churches and ancient buildings.
- Football, rugby and cricket are popular sports.

What am I?

- I am green. Mostly I have white flowers.
- I usually have 3 leaves.
- Ancient people thought I was magical.
- I am strongly associated with Ireland.

What am I?

Answers at the back of the atlas.

Try this!

Many different sports are popular in the United Kingdom. Look at the map and find

- 3 sports played with a ball
- 1 sport that takes place on water
- 2 sports that need ice or snow

Answers at the back of the atlas.

Shetland Islands

Orkney Islands

A t l a n t i c

O c e a n

Outer Hebrides

Lewis

The Minch

Inner Hebrides

Skye

golden eagle

Highland cattle

Moray Firth

Inverness ○

Loch Ness

skiing

oil rig

Aberdeen ○

fishing boat

Ben Nevis

Fort William ○

Grampian Mts

S C O T L A N D

Highland piper

curling

Dundee ○

Edinburgh ○

Firth of Forth

Edinburgh Castle

Glasgow ○

Jura

Islay

N o r t h

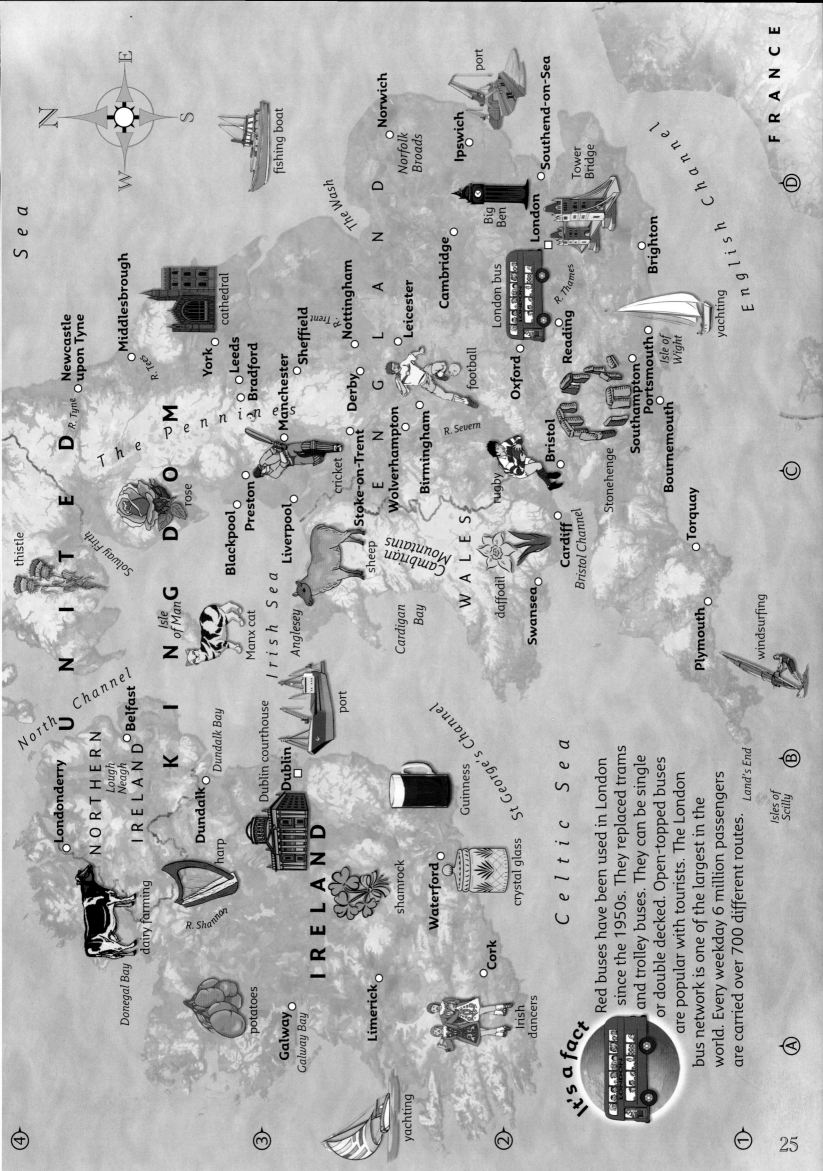

Sea

N
E
W
S

fishing boat

UNITED

North Channel

Londonderry

NORTHERN

IRELAND

Belfast

Lough
Neagh

KING

Dundalk

Dundalk Bay

harp

Dublin courthouse

Dublin

port

IRELAND

R. Shannon

dairy farming

Donegal Bay

potatoes

Galway

Galway Bay

Limerick

Waterford

crystal glass

Cork

shamrock

Guinness

St George's Channel

Irish
dancers

Celtic Sea

Isle of Man
Manx cat

Irish Sea

Anglesey

Cardigan
Bay

sheep

Cambrian
Mountains

WALES

daffodil

Cardiff

Bristol Channel

Swansea

thistle

Solway Firth

rose

The Pennines

Blackpool

Preston

Liverpool

Stoke-on-Trent

cricket

Manchester

R. Tees

Middlesbrough

cathedral

York

Leeds

Bradford

Sheffield

Derby

Nottingham

Leicester

ENGLAND

R. Trent

Wolverhampton

Birmingham

R. Severn

rugby

Bristol

Stonehenge

football

Cambridge

Oxford

Reading

R. Thames

London bus

Southampton

Portsmouth

Isle of
Wight

Bournemouth

Torquay

Plymouth

windsurfing

Land's End

Isles of
Scilly

Newcastle
upon Tyne

R. Tyne

DOM

The Wash

Norwich

Norfolk
Broads

Ipswich

port

Big
Ben

London

Southend-on-Sea

Tower
Bridge

Brighton

yachting

English Channel

FRANCE

yachting

A B C D

1 2 3 4

25

Northern Europe

glaciers

Reykjavik

ICELAND

Northern Europe has a rugged landscape and many of its countries are almost completely surrounded by sea. In the far north winters can be extremely cold and the seas may freeze for several months. Most people live in the south of this region where the climate is milder.

Faroe Is (Denmark)

Did you know?

- The Baltic Sea borders on 9 countries. Parts of it can be frozen for 6 months of the year.

- Brittany is a region in northwest France. The people there speak Breton.

- Puppets are popular in the Czech Republic. They are used to entertain people and tell stories.

- German is spoken in Austria, Switzerland and Germany.

What am I?

- I have large round eyes, a sharp beak and claws.

- I fly about at night and I sleep during the day.

- I hunt small animals, insects and fish.

- I build nests in trees, barns and sometimes underground.

What am I?

Try this!

Many different types of food are grown or manufactured in this region. Look at the map and find

1 type of cheese
3 types of farm animal
1 type of pastry

Answers at the back of the atlas.

salmon

fishing boats

oil rigs

Norwegian church

DENM

Highland piper

Edinburgh Castle

shamrock

IRELAND

UNITED

harp

Dublin

sheep

North Sea

pigs

KINGDOM

rugby

Tower Bridge

windmills

NETHERLANDS

Amsterdam
The Hague

Gouda cheese

London

Atlantic Ocean

English Channel

Brussels

BELGIUM

R. Rhine

G E R

Frankfurt

LUXEMBOURG

Mont St Michel

Paris

Luxembourg

R. Loire

Arc de Triomphe

Eiffel Tower

R. Seine

owl

seafood

Bay of Biscay

F R A N C E

croissants

Massif Central

Bern

SWITZERLAND

I T A L

Arctic Ocean

blue whale

puffin

eider duck

owl

Lappland

Kola Peninsula

lemming

reindeer

wild mushrooms

fishing through ice

moose

Gulf of Bothnia

White Sea

wheat farming

R. Northern Dvina

paper making

lynx

FINLAND

Lake Onega

R U S S I A N

skiing

saunas

Lake Ladoga

St Petersburg

beavers

R. Sukhona

Oslo

Winter Palace

wild horses

Helsinki

F E D E R A T I O N

Vänern

Stockholm

Tallinn

dairy cows

Vättern

ESTONIA

badger

LATVIA

Moscow

Volga Uplands

Riga

Plain

Kremlin

R. Dvina

Copenhagen

LITHUANIA

Central Russian

wind farms

Vilnius

potatoes

R. Dnieper

RUS. FED.

Russian dolls

R. Elbe

North European

Uplands

Berlin

R. Vistula

Minsk

It's a fact

boar

B E L A R U S

Warsaw

MANY

P O L A N D

Glass is made from sand. The sand is heated to a high temperature until it melts. Many items we use every day are made from glass. It is transparent – we can see through it. Sometimes metals are added to glass to change its colour. Brightly coloured stained glass is often found in church windows.

glass making

brown bears

football

Prague

U K R A I N E

CZECH REPUBLIC

Carpathian Mts

R. Dniester

SLOVAKIA

MOLDOVA

Bratislava

Munich

Vienna

R. Danube

Budapest

Chisinau

castle

S

castle

AUSTRIA

HUNGARY

ROMANIA

Y

Ⓓ

Ⓔ

Ⓕ

27

Southern Europe

DENMARK

North Sea

5

UNITED KINGDOM
The Hague
London

NETHERLANDS
Amsterdam

Hamburg

Hannover

Berlin

R. Rhine

G E R M A N Y

Brussels

BELGIUM

Cologne

Frankfurt

LUXEMBOURG

English Channel

4

Atlantic Ocean

apples
R. Loire

Paris

Eiffel Tower

Arc de Triomphe

F R A N C E

croissants

Swiss cheese

football

castle

Munich

seafood

Bay of Biscay

wine

cheese

Massif Central

grapes

Bern

SWITZERLAND

LIECHTENSTEIN

Mont Blanc

cathedral

gondola

AUST

swordfish

Cantabrian Mts

garlic

skiing

Mont Blanc

Milan

R. Rhône

R. Po

Oporto

bull fighting

skiing

ANDORRA

Marseille

MONACO

Apennines

cars

SAN MARINO

P O R T U G A L

Spanish guitar

Pyrenees

3

R. Tagus

Madrid

leather goods

Barcelona

port

casinos

Leaning Tower of Pisa

Rome Vatican

Lisbon

S P A I N

beaches

Balearic Islands

cruise ships

Sardinia

Colosseum

sardines

oranges

flamenco dancers

almonds

grapes

Tyrrhenian Sea

Strait of Gibraltar

M e d i t e

Sicily

2

MOROCCO

A L G E R I A

TUNISIA

The south of this region lies on the shores of the warm
Mediterranean Sea where many people spend their holidays.
Southern Europe and Africa are separated by only 15 kilometres
(9 miles) of water known as the Strait of Gibraltar, which links the
Atlantic Ocean and the Mediterranean Sea. Two of the world's
smallest countries, Vatican City and Monaco, are in Southern Europe.

1

A   F   R

Ⓐ

Ⓑ

Ⓒ

It's a fact

A gondola is a traditional, long, narrow rowing boat used for transport on the canals in Venice. It is made from 8 different types of wood and is always painted black. Only one oar is used to push a gondola forward in the water.

Warsaw

POLAND

cathedral

Kiev

UKRAINE

Prague
CZECH REPUBLIC

glass making

brown bears

R. Dniester

SLOVAKIA

MOLDOVA

Vienna

Bratislava

HUNGARY

Chisinau

RIA

Budapest

SLOVENIA

Hungarian church

Ljubljana

Zagreb

castle

CROATIA

ROMANIA

Croatian house

Belgrade

Bucharest

BOSNIA-HERZEGOVINA

R. Danube

roses

Black Sea

Sarajevo

SERBIA

Balkan Mts

grapes

MONTENEGRO

Sofia

Adriatic Sea

Podgorica

ALBANIA

Skopje

BULGARIA

Istanbul

Tirana

MACEDONIA

fortress

pizza

Naples

Greek pottery

TURKEY

spaghetti

olives

GREECE

Izmir

Greek church

Aegean Sea

kebabs

Athens

Parthenon

Ionian Sea

volcano

Valletta

MALTA

Cretan mosque

Crete

Knossos

fishing boats

a n e a n S e a

LIBYA

EGYPT

ICA

Did you know?

- The islands of Sicily and Sardinia belong to Italy.

- Venice is built on a large area of water, called a lagoon.

- In Albania and Bulgaria nodding your head means no. Shaking your head from side to side means yes.

- In France April Fool's Day is known as April Fish Day.

- Portugal has the world's largest solar powered electricity plant.

- The wristwatch was invented in Switzerland.

- The River Danube flows through 7 countries.

What am I?

- I am made from flour, and egg or water.

- I am cooked quickly in boiling water.

- I am often covered in tomato sauce.

- My name means 'thin string'.

- I am a type of pasta.

What am I?

Answers at the back of the atlas.

Try this!

Many famous buidings and ruins are found in this region.
Look at the map and find

Arc de Triomphe
Colosseum
Knossos
Parthenon
Leaning Tower of Pisa

Asia

Asia is the largest continent. It is bigger than Europe and Africa combined. Asia extends from the Ural mountains to the Pacific Ocean in the east and from the Arctic Ocean to the Indian Ocean in the south. Climates vary from the cold Arctic in the north to hot tropical in the south.

Try this!

This country is also an island. Can you name it?

Answers at the back of the atlas.

⑤

④

③

②

①

Arctic

N
W E
S

Ural Mountains

S i b

Moscow

E U R O P E

RUSSIAN FEDERATION

Black Sea

CYPRUS

Ankara

GEORGIA

T'bilisi

Yerevan

AZERBAIJAN

Baku

Astana

LEBANON

TURKEY

UZBEKISTAN

KAZAKHSTAN

Bishkek

ISRAEL

SYRIA

ARMENIA

Caspian Sea

TURKMENISTAN

Tashkent

KYRGYZSTAN

Damascus

Amman

Baghdad

Tehran

Ashgabat

Dushanbe

TAJIKISTAN

Kunlun Shan

JORDAN

IRAQ

IRAN

Kabul

Islamabad

Plateau of Tibet

BAHRAIN

Kuwait KUWAIT

AFGHANISTAN

Himalaya

QATAR

SAUDI ARABIA

Riyadh

The Gulf

New Delhi

NEPAL

Kathmandu

Mount Everest

BHUTAN

Thimphu

UNITED ARAB EMIRATES

Muscat

PAKISTAN

Dhaka

Red Sea

San'a

OMAN

MYANMAR (BURMA)

A F R I C A

YEMEN

INDIA

BANGLADESH

Naypyidaw

Socotra (Yemen)

Arabian Sea

Bay of Bengal

Yangon (Rangoon)

Andaman Is (India)

SRI LANKA

Nicobar Is (India)

MALDIVES

Sri Jayewardenepura Kotte

I n d i a n   O c e a n

Ⓐ

Ⓑ

Ⓒ

People facts

- Population: 4 085 000 000 (including Russian Federation)
- Country with most people: China 1 323 345 000
- City with most people: Tokyo 35 327 000

Geography facts

- Area: 45 036 492 square kilometres (17 388 686 square miles)
- Largest country: Russian Federation 17 075 400 square kilometres (6 592 849 square miles)
- Longest river: Chang Jiang 6380 kilometres (3964 miles)
- Highest mountain: Mount Everest 8848 metres (29 028 feet)
- Largest lake: Caspian Sea 371 000 square kilometres (143 243 square miles)
- Largest island: Borneo 745 561 square kilometres (287 863 square miles)

Did you know?

- More than half of the world's people live in Asia.
- Lake Baikal, in Siberia, is the deepest lake in the world.
- The Chinese invented paper, ink, the compass and silk.
- Indonesia has more active volcanoes than any other country.
- The Dead Sea is so salty bathers can float on top of the water.
- The Siberian tiger is the largest living cat in the world.
- The red dot in the centre of the Japanese flag represents a red sun.

Ocean

Bering Sea

Sea of Okhotsk

e r i a

Lake Baikal

Sea of Japan (East Sea)

Ulan Bator

MONGOLIA

NORTH KOREA

JAPAN

Pyongyang

Tokyo

Beijing

Seoul

SOUTH KOREA

CHINA

East China Sea

Chang Jiang

Pacific

Ocean

T'aipei

TAIWAN

Hanoi

LAOS

Vientiane

South China Sea

Manila

PALAU

Bangkok

CAMBODIA

PHILIPPINES

Melekeok

Phnom Penh

VIETNAM

BRUNEI

THAILAND

Bandar Seri Begawan

Kuala Lumpur

MALAYSIA

Borneo

Putrajaya

Singapore

SINGAPORE

INDONESIA

EAST TIMOR

O C E A N I A

Jakarta

Dili

Ⓓ   Ⓔ   Ⓕ

Russian Federation

⑤

Russia is the largest country in the world. It has borders with 14 different countries. Most Russians live in the west of the country. Siberia, in the north, is almost empty. It is dry and extremely cold there. The southwest, on the coast of the Black Sea, is very warm. Much of the country is covered with huge grassy plains, known as steppes.

Baltic Sea

FINLAND

reindeer

Barents Sea

fishing in the Arctic

Kara Sea

eider duck

④

POLAND

potatoes

RUS. FED.

ESTONIA

LITHUANIA

LATVIA

St Petersburg

ice hockey

Archangel

R. Pechora

Ural owl

Vorkuta

lynx

Sib...

vodka

BELARUS

gymnastics

Kremlin

R. North Dvina

R. Yenisey

R. Dniestr

MOLDOVA

Kiev

UKRAINE

football

Moscow

Nizhniy Novgorod

ballet

Perm

R. Ob

R U S S I A

R. Lower Tunguska

③

F E D E R A T I...

West Siberian Plain

Sea of Azov

R. Don

sugarbeet

R. Volga

wheat

Kazan

Yekaterinburg

Samara

Ufa

chess

cathedral

Cossack dancers

R. Yenisey

R. Irtysh

Volgograd

balalaika

Black Sea

TURKEY

②

GEORGIA

ARMENIA

AZ.

AZERBAIJAN

Caspian seal

Caspian Sea

Russian dolls

Chelyabinsk

Omsk

cathedral

Novosibirsk

Krasnoyarsk

brown bear

K A Z A K H S T A N

Astana

Siberian stag

Aral Sea

UZBEKISTAN

TURKMENISTAN

rocket launch site

R. Syrdarya

wheat

Lake Balkhash

MONGOL...

I R A N

①

Ashgabat

R. Amudarya

Tashkent

Bishkek

KYRGYZSTAN

TAJIKISTAN

Ⓐ

AFGHANISTAN

Ⓑ

C **C H I**

Ⓒ

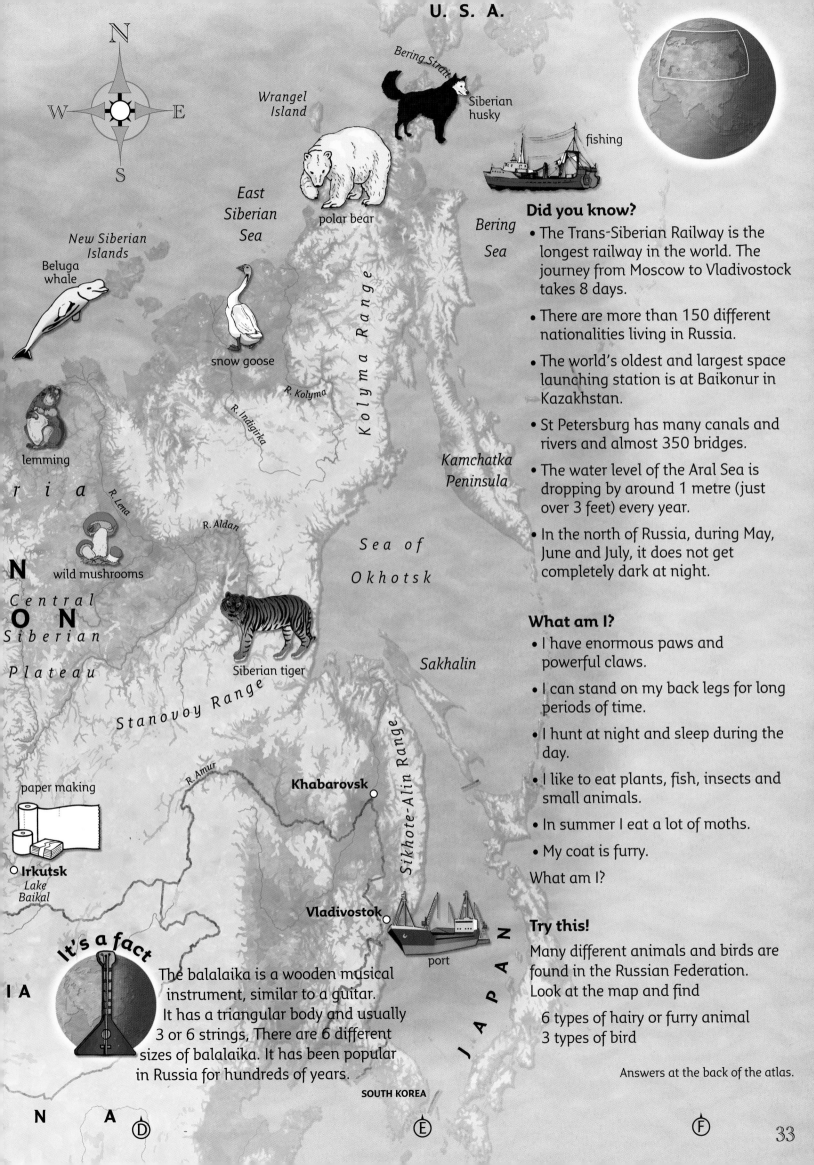

U. S. A.

Bering Strait

Wrangel Island

Siberian husky

fishing

East Siberian Sea

polar bear

Bering Sea

New Siberian Islands

Beluga whale

snow goose

R. Kolyma

R. Indigirka

K o l y m a   R a n g e

Kamchatka Peninsula

lemming

R. Lena

R. Aldan

S e a   o f   O k h o t s k

wild mushrooms

N

C e n t r a l

O N

S i b e r i a n

P l a t e a u

Siberian tiger

Sakhalin

S t a n o v o y   R a n g e

R. Amur

Sikhote-Alin Range

paper making

Khabarovsk

Vladivostok

port

○ **Irkutsk**
Lake Baikal

J A P A N

It's a fact

The balalaika is a wooden musical instrument, similar to a guitar. It has a triangular body and usually 3 or 6 strings, There are 6 different sizes of balalaika. It has been popular in Russia for hundreds of years.

I A

SOUTH KOREA

N   **A**   Ⓓ

Did you know?

- The Trans-Siberian Railway is the longest railway in the world. The journey from Moscow to Vladivostock takes 8 days.

- There are more than 150 different nationalities living in Russia.

- The world's oldest and largest space launching station is at Baikonur in Kazakhstan.

- St Petersburg has many canals and rivers and almost 350 bridges.

- The water level of the Aral Sea is dropping by around 1 metre (just over 3 feet) every year.

- In the north of Russia, during May, June and July, it does not get completely dark at night.

What am I?

- I have enormous paws and powerful claws.

- I can stand on my back legs for long periods of time.

- I hunt at night and sleep during the day.

- I like to eat plants, fish, insects and small animals.

- In summer I eat a lot of moths.

- My coat is furry.

What am I?

Try this!

Many different animals and birds are found in the Russian Federation. Look at the map and find

6 types of hairy or furry animal
3 types of bird

Answers at the back of the atlas.

Ⓔ   Ⓕ   33

Southwest Asia

Black Sea

⑤

GREECE

The north and west of this area is mountainous, with high ranges extending through Turkey into Iran. The Arabian Peninsula between the Red Sea and The Gulf is mostly dry sandy desert. Water is scarce in much of Southwest Asia. Two major rivers are the Tigris and Euphrates.

④

LIBYA

Mediterranean Sea

Did you know?

- Saudi Arabia is the world's leading exporter of oil.

- Three of the world's major religions started in this area: Judaism, Christianity and Islam.

- Damascus, the capital of Syria, is one of the oldest cities in the world.

- The Caucasus mountain range protects Armenia, Georgia and Azerbaijan from cold north winds.

③

What am I?

- I am a type of bird.

- I have long, thin legs and a long neck.

- I like to wade in shallow water.

- I often stand on one leg.

- I eat small shrimps.

- I am pink.

What am I?

②

Try this!

Look at the map. Can you find these:

3 Arabian animals
1 religious building
1 sport popular in Pakistan

Answers at the back of the atlas.

①

El'brus

GEORGIA

kebabs

■ **Ankara**

mosque

ARMENIA
Yerevan

coffee

T U R K E Y

Taurus Mts

Crusader castles

cedar trees

Nicosia □

CYPRUS

SYRIA

date palms

Beirut □

LEBANON

Damascus □

ISRAEL

Amman □ **JORDAN**

Jerusalem

Syrian Desert

Baghdad □
R. Tigris
R. Euphrates

□ **Cairo**

Sphinx

Dome of the Rock

oil refineries

I R A Q

Arabian fox

An Nafud

carpets

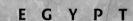
desert safari

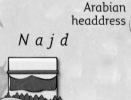
Bedouin tent

E G Y P T

Arabian headdress

Najd

scuba diving

Riyadh

crocodile

R. Nile

R. Nile

Muslim praying at Mecca

S A U D I

angel fish

Red Sea

Asir

Arabian horse

S U D A N

Arabian horse

E R I T R E A

dhow

San'a □

Y E M

Ⓐ

Ras Dejen

Ⓑ

E T H I O P I A

Ⓒ **DJIBOUTI** *Gulf*

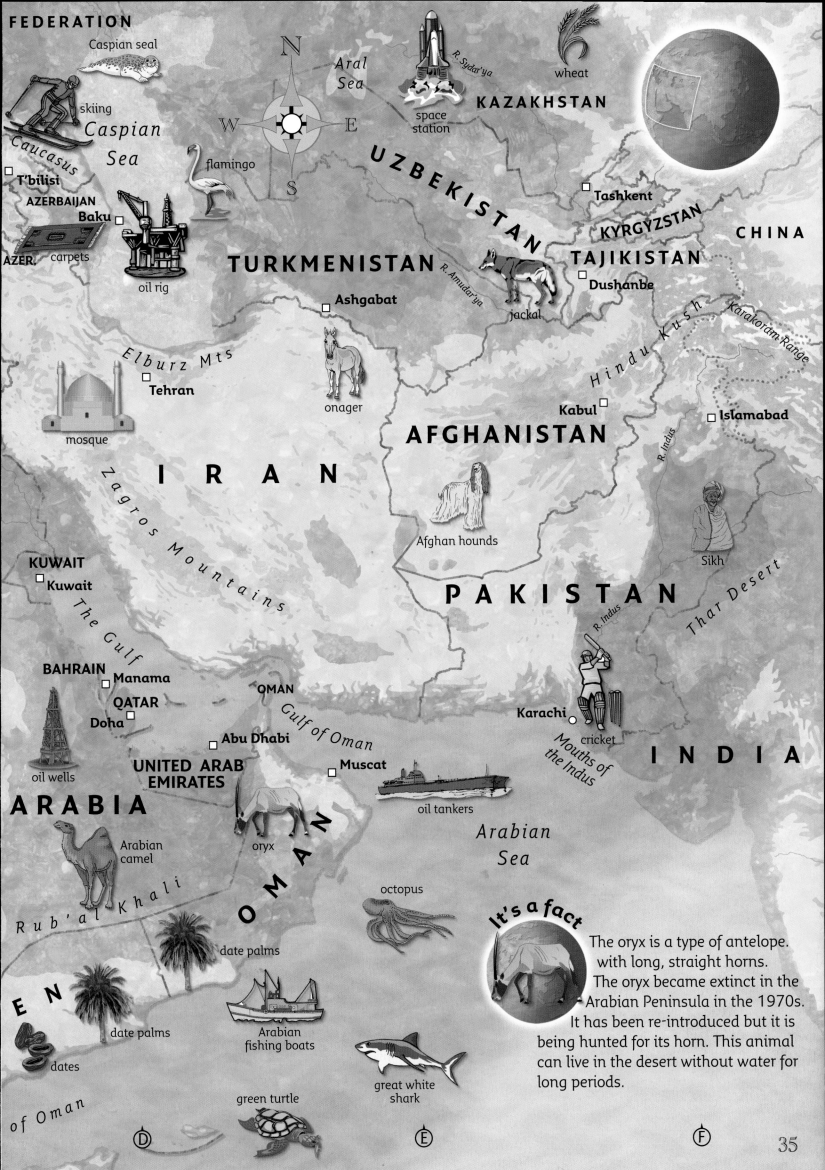

FEDERATION

Caspian seal

skiing

Caspian Sea

Caucasus

□ T'bilisi

AZERBAIJAN

Baku □

AZER. carpets

flamingo

oil rig

N
W E
S

Aral Sea

space station

R. Sydar'ya

wheat

KAZAKHSTAN

UZBEKISTAN

□ Tashkent

KYRGYZSTAN

TAJIKISTAN

CHINA

R. Amudar'ya

jackal

□ Dushanbe

Elburz Mts

□ Ashgabat

TURKMENISTAN

□ **Tehran**

mosque

onager

Hindu Kush

Karakoram Range

Kabul □

AFGHANISTAN

□ **Islamabad**

R. Indus

I R A N

Zagros Mountains

KUWAIT

□ **Kuwait**

The Gulf

BAHRAIN

□ **Manama**

QATAR

Doha □

oil wells

A R A B I A

Arabian camel

Rub' al Khali

E N

dates

date palms

date palms

Arabian fishing boats

□ **Abu Dhabi**

UNITED ARAB EMIRATES

oryx

□ **Muscat**

Afghan hounds

P A K I S T A N

Sikh

Thar Desert

R. Indus

cricket

Karachi ○

Mouths of the Indus

I N D I A

Gulf of Oman

O M A N

oil tankers

Arabian Sea

octopus

green turtle

great white shark

of Oman

It's a fact

The oryx is a type of antelope. with long, straight horns. The oryx became extinct in the Arabian Peninsula in the 1970s. It has been re-introduced but it is being hunted for its horn. This animal can live in the desert without water for long periods.

Ⓓ Ⓔ Ⓕ

35

South Asia

South Asia is a region of contrasting landscapes and weather. In the north is the great mountain range of Himalaya where the climate is harsh and few people live. The lands at the mouths of the Ganges river are low lying and flooding occurs during the heavy rains in the monsoon season. Most people live in the river valleys, plains and big cities.

What am I?

- I live in the sea, espec[...] coral reefs.
- I have 3 hearts and m[...]
- My soft body means th[...] squeeze through smal[...]
- I have a beak.
- I have 8 arms.

What am I?

Try this!

Many different animals[...] are found in this region. Look at the map and fin[...]

3 members of the cat f[...]
2 types of bird
1 type of animal with s[...]

Answers at[...]

Tibetan monks

Lhasa

Thimphu
BHUTAN

Mount Everest

NEPAL

Nepalese temple

Kathmandu

Patna

Indian rhinoceros

R. Ganges

BANGLADESH

R. Brahmaput[...]

yak

Plateau of Tibet

K u n l u n   S h a n

C H I N A

*H
i
m
a
l
a
y
a*

K2

Kashmir stag

snow leopard

mountain goat

Golden Temple, Amritsar

Delhi
New Delhi

Taj Mahal

Jaipur

Lahore

Islamabad

Faisalabad

T h a r   D e s e r t

Sikh

R. Indus

H i n d u   K u s h

Kabul

Dushanbe

TAJIKISTAN

jackal

[...]GHANISTAN

[P]AKISTAN

[Afg]han hound

N
W — E
S

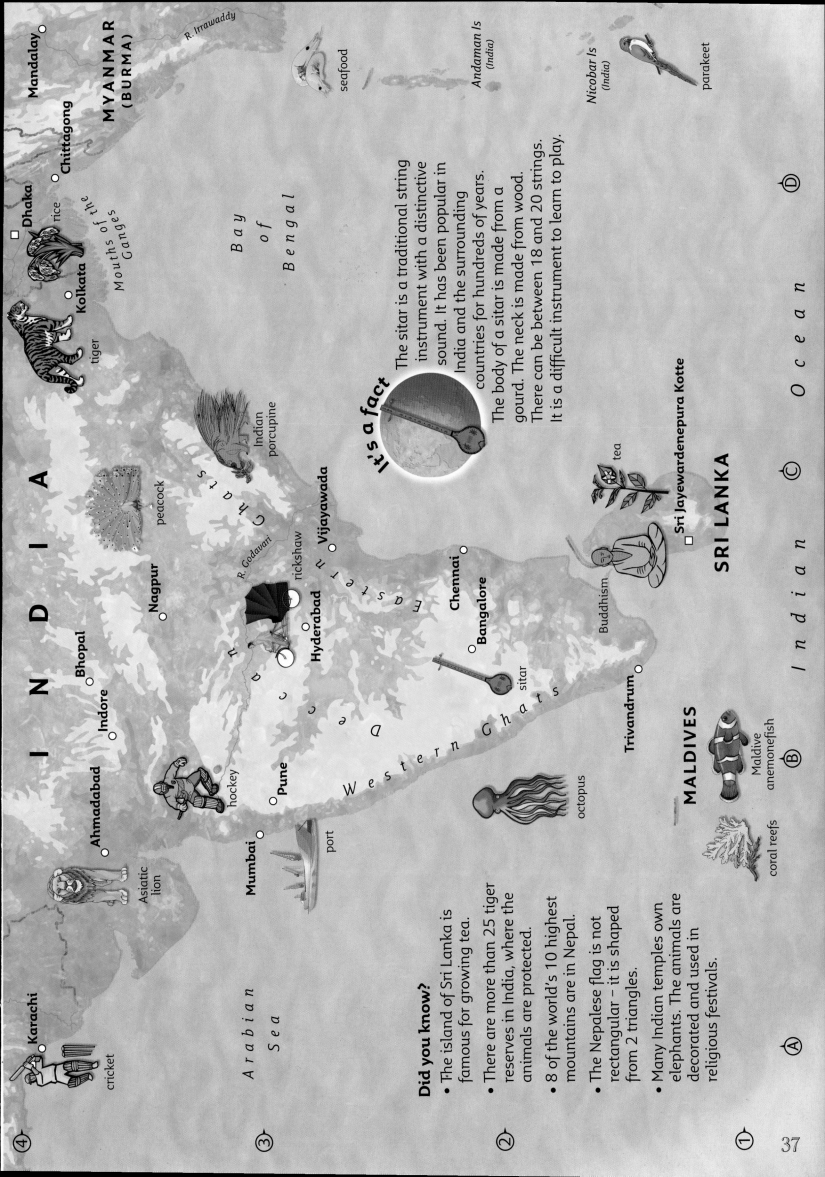

INDIA

MYANMAR (BURMA)

Mandalay

Chittagong

Dhaka

rice

R. Irrawaddy

Mouths of the Ganges

Kolkata

tiger

seafood

Andaman Is *(India)*

Bay of Bengal

Nicobar Is *(India)*

parakeet

Indian porcupine

peacock

Eastern Ghats

R. Godavari

Vijayawada

rickshaw

Nagpur

Bhopal

Indore

Ahmadabad

Karachi

cricket

Asiatic lion

Hyderabad

Deccan

Chennai

Bangalore

sitar

tea

Sri Jayewardenepura Kotte

SRI LANKA

Buddhism

Mumbai

port

Pune

octopus

Western Ghats

Trivandrum

MALDIVES

Maldive anemonefish

coral reefs

Arabian Sea

hockey

Indian Ocean

It's a fact

The sitar is a traditional string instrument with a distinctive sound. It has been popular in India and the surrounding countries for hundreds of years. The body of a sitar is made from a gourd. The neck is made from wood. There can be between 18 and 20 strings. It is a difficult instrument to learn to play.

Did you know?

• The island of Sri Lanka is famous for growing tea.

• There are more than 25 tiger reserves in India, where the animals are protected.

• 8 of the world's 10 highest mountains are in Nepal.

• The Nepalese flag is not rectangular – it is shaped from 2 triangles.

• Many Indian temples own elephants. The animals are decorated and used in religious festivals.

Ⓐ Ⓑ Ⓒ Ⓓ

④ ③ ② ①

China and Japan

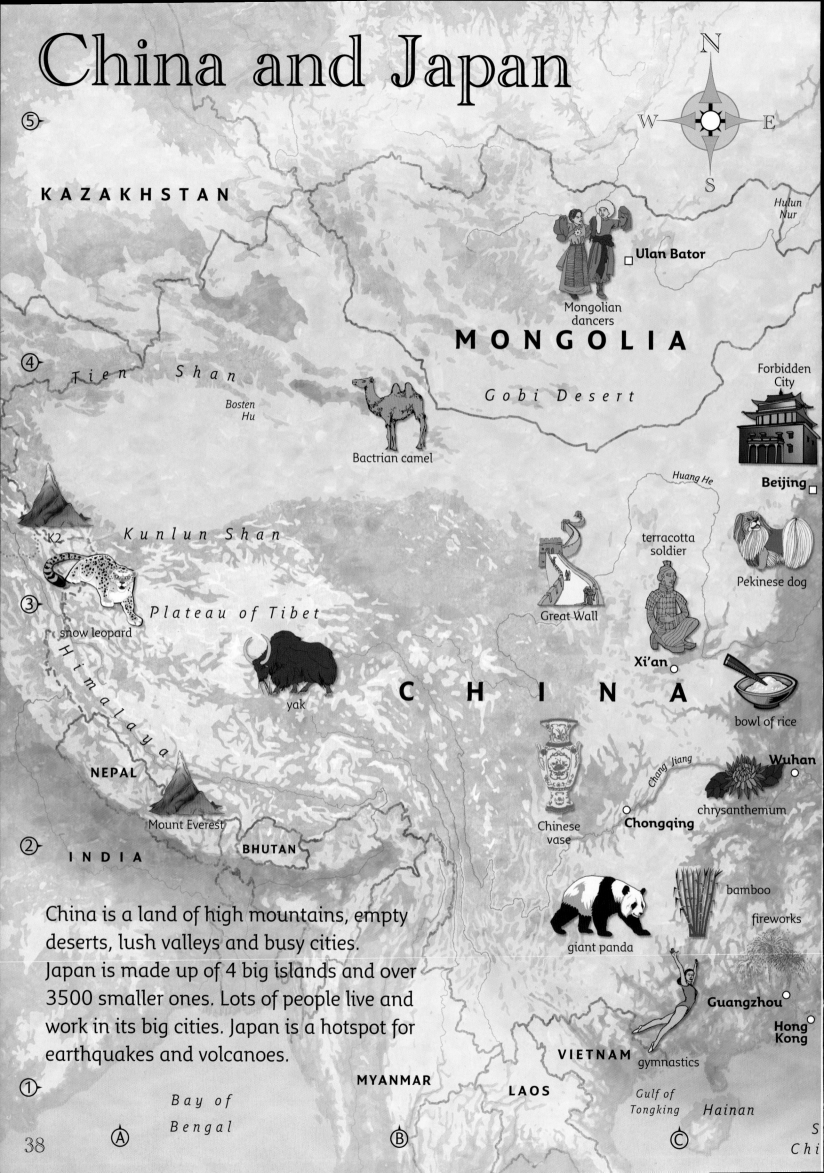

KAZAKHSTAN

N
W   E
S

Hulun Nur

Mongolian dancers

■ **Ulan Bator**

MONGOLIA

④

Tien Shan

Bosten Hu

Gobi Desert

Forbidden City

Bactrian camel

Huang He

■ **Beijing**

K2

Kunlun Shan

terracotta soldier

Pekinese dog

snow leopard

Plateau of Tibet

Great Wall

③

Himalaya

yak

C H I N A

Xi'an ○

bowl of rice

NEPAL

Mount Everest

Chinese vase

Chang Jiang

Wuhan ○

chrysanthemum

Chongqing

② **INDIA**

BHUTAN

China is a land of high mountains, empty deserts, lush valleys and busy cities. Japan is made up of 4 big islands and over 3500 smaller ones. Lots of people live and work in its big cities. Japan is a hotspot for earthquakes and volcanoes.

giant panda

bamboo

fireworks

Guangzhou ○

Hong Kong

VIETNAM

gymnastics

①

MYANMAR

LAOS

Gulf of Tongking

Hainan

Ⓐ

Bay of Bengal

Ⓑ

Ⓒ

S Chi

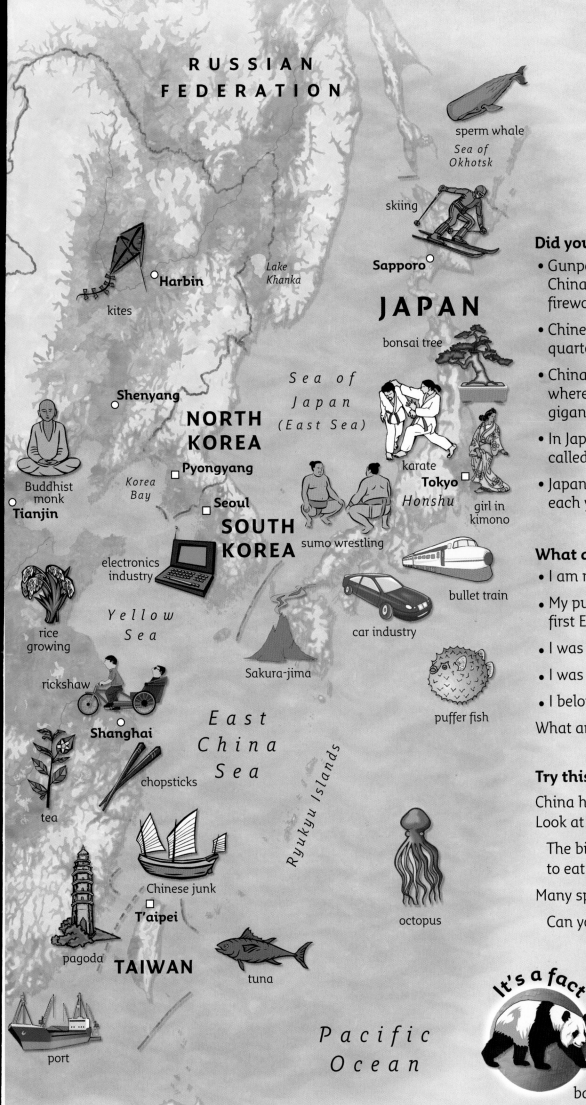

RUSSIAN FEDERATION

sperm whale
Sea of Okhotsk

skiing

Sapporo

JAPAN

bonsai tree

Harbin

kites

Lake Khanka

karate

Buddhist monk

Shenyang

Sea of Japan (East Sea)

NORTH KOREA

Pyongyang

Korea Bay

Tianjin

Seoul

SOUTH KOREA

sumo wrestling

Tokyo

Honshu

girl in kimono

electronics industry

Yellow Sea

rice growing

rickshaw

Sakura-jima

bullet train

car industry

puffer fish

Shanghai

East China Sea

chopsticks

tea

Ryukyu Islands

Chinese junk

T'aipei

octopus

pagoda

TAIWAN

tuna

port

Pacific Ocean

outh na Sea

PHILIPPINES

Ⓓ

Ⓔ

Did you know?

- Gunpowder was first discovered in China. It can be used to make fireworks and signal flares.

- Chinese is spoken by almost a quarter of all the people in the world.

- China is one of the few countries where fossils of 'Big Foot' (homo gigantus) have been found.

- In Japan the green traffic light is called 'blue'.

- Japan has about 1500 earthquakes each year.

What am I?

- I am made of baked earth.

- My purpose was to protect the first Emperor in the afterlife.

- I was buried in 210-109 BC.

- I was discovered in 1974.

- I belonged to an army.

What am I?

Try this!

China has many different animals. Look at the map and find

The big furry animal who loves to eat bamboo.

Many sports are played in Japan

Can you name 2 of these?

Answers at the back of the atlas.

It's a fact

The giant panda has lived in bamboo forests for several million years. Each year a panda can eat 5 tonnes of bamboo. There are only about 1600 left in the wild.

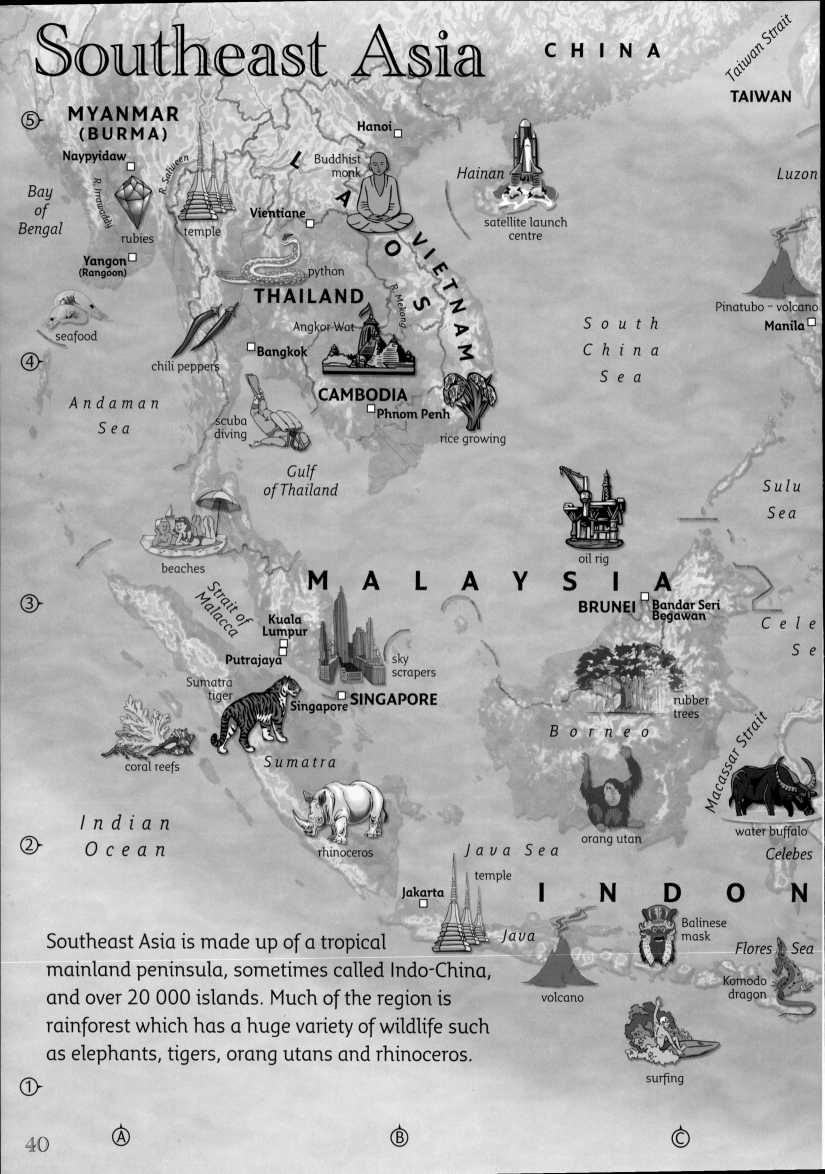

Southeast Asia

CHINA

Taiwan Strait

TAIWAN

⑤ **MYANMAR (BURMA)**

Naypyidaw

R. Irrawaddy

R. Salween

Hanoi

Buddhist monk

Hainan

Luzon

Bay of Bengal

rubies

temple

Vientiane

satellite launch centre

Yangon (Rangoon)

python

THAILAND

R. Mekong

L A O S

V I E T N A M

South China Sea

Pinatubo – volcano

Manila

seafood

Angkor Wat

chili peppers

④

Bangkok

Andaman Sea

scuba diving

CAMBODIA

Phnom Penh

rice growing

Gulf of Thailand

oil rig

Sulu Sea

beaches

M A L A Y S I A

③ *Strait of Malacca*

Kuala Lumpur

BRUNEI

Bandar Seri Begawan

Cele Se

Putrajaya

sky scrapers

Sumatra tiger

rubber trees

Singapore **SINGAPORE**

coral reefs

Sumatra

B o r n e o

Macassar Strait

orang utan

water buffalo

② *Indian Ocean*

rhinoceros

Java Sea

Celebes

temple

Jakarta

I N D O N

Balinese mask

Southeast Asia is made up of a tropical mainland peninsula, sometimes called Indo-China, and over 20 000 islands. Much of the region is rainforest which has a huge variety of wildlife such as elephants, tigers, orang utans and rhinoceros.

Java

volcano

Flores Sea

Komodo dragon

surfing

① ④ Ⓑ Ⓒ

T'aipei

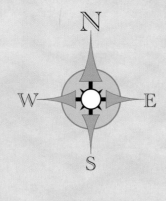
tuna

N
W E
S

Pacific

Strait

Ocean

Luzon

It's a fact

Many rubber tree plantations are found in Southeast Asia. When rubber trees are 5-6 years old they produce latex, collected from slits made in the tree trunk. Latex is made into rubber. The trees produce latex for 20-25 years. They are then cut down and the wood is used to make furniture.

Did you know?

- Singapore is made up of 63 islands.
- The western half of New Guinea is part of Indonesia.
- There are around 150 active volcanoes in Indonesia.
- The Sumatran tiger is the smallest tiger. It is a very fast swimmer.
- A cowrie is the shell of a snail that lives in the sea in tropical areas.

PHILIPPINES

oyster and pearl

Mindanao

pineapples

□ **Melekeok**

PALAU

What am I?

- I am a type of lizard.
- I am only found in central Indonesia.
- I have a long body, sharp teeth and strong claws.
- My tongue is long and yellow.
- I am sometimes known as a dragon.

What am I?

b e s

a

clams

Molucca Sea

manta ray

Try this!

2 water sports are shown on the map. Can you name them?

Answers at the back of the atlas.

coral reefs

coconut palm tree

New Guinea

Puncak Jaya

PAPUA NEW

E S I A

Banda Sea

cowrie shell

GUINEA

rubber trees

Dili
□ **EAST TIMOR**

Arafura Sea

Coral Sea

A U S T R A L I A

Ⓓ   Ⓔ   Ⓕ   41

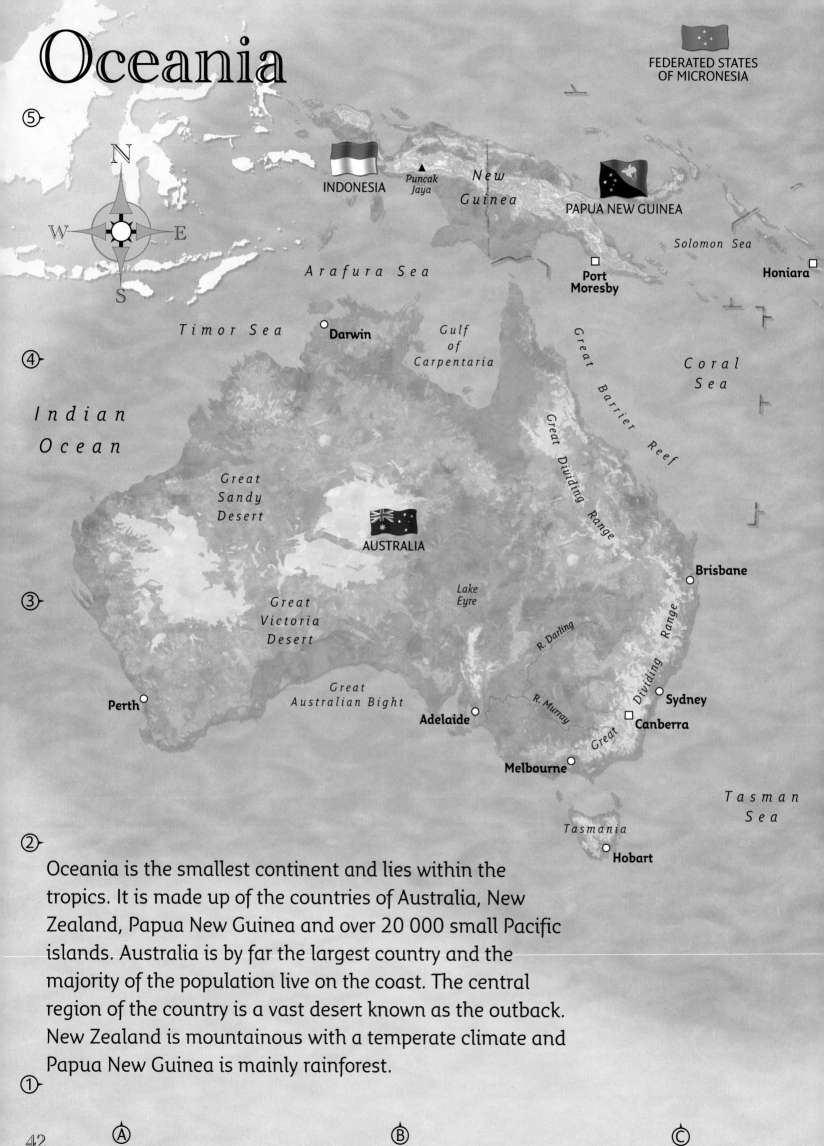

Oceania

⑤

N
W E
S

FEDERATED STATES
OF MICRONESIA

INDONESIA

▲ *Puncak Jaya*

New Guinea

PAPUA NEW GUINEA

Solomon Sea

Honiara

Arafura Sea

□ **Port Moresby**

④

Timor Sea

○ **Darwin**

Gulf of Carpentaria

Coral Sea

Great Barrier Reef

Indian Ocean

Great Sandy Desert

Great Dividing Range

AUSTRALIA

③

Great Victoria Desert

Lake Eyre

Brisbane ○

R. Darling

Dividing Range

Great Australian Bight

○ **Perth**

Adelaide ○

R. Murray

Great

Sydney ○

□ **Canberra**

Melbourne ○

Tasman Sea

Tasmania

② **Hobart** ○

Oceania is the smallest continent and lies within the tropics. It is made up of the countries of Australia, New Zealand, Papua New Guinea and over 20 000 small Pacific islands. Australia is by far the largest country and the majority of the population live on the coast. The central region of the country is a vast desert known as the outback. New Zealand is mountainous with a temperate climate and Papua New Guinea is mainly rainforest.

①

Ⓐ Ⓑ Ⓒ

Bairiki

Yaren

NAURU

KIRIBATI

SOLOMON
ISLANDS

TUVALU

Vaiaku

VANUATU

Wallis and
Futuna Islands
(France)

SAMOA

Port Vila

Apia

American
Samoa
(USA)

Suva

TONGA

New
Caledonia
(France)

Nouméa

FIJI

Nuku'alofa

Niue
(New
Zealand)

Cook
Islands
(New
Zealand)

FRENCH
POLYNESIA

Pacific

Ocean

Auckland

North
Island

NEW
ZEALAND

Wellington

South
Island

Did you know?

- 40% of Australia is covered by sand dunes.

- Australia's Great Barrier Reef is the world's largest coral reef.

- In South Island, New Zealand, there are 18 peaks of more than 3000 metres (9842 feet).

- The stars on the flags of Oceanic countries represent the Southern Cross constellation.

- Kangaroos are only found in Australia and New Guinea but there are over 40 different types.

People facts

- Population: 33 000 000

- Country with most people: Australia 20 155 000

- City with most people: Sydney 4 388 000

Geography facts

- Area: 8 844 516 square kilometres (3 414 887 square miles)

- Largest country: Australia 7 692 024 square kilometres (2 969 907 square miles)

- Longest river: Murray-Darling 3750 kilometres (2330 miles)

- Highest mountain: Puncak Jaya 5030 metres (16 502 feet)

- Largest lake: Lake Eyre 0-8900 square kilometres (0-3436 square miles)

- Largest island: New Guinea 808 510 square kilometres (312 167 square miles)

Try this!

Which countries do these flags belong to?

Answers at the back of the atlas.

Australia & New Zealand

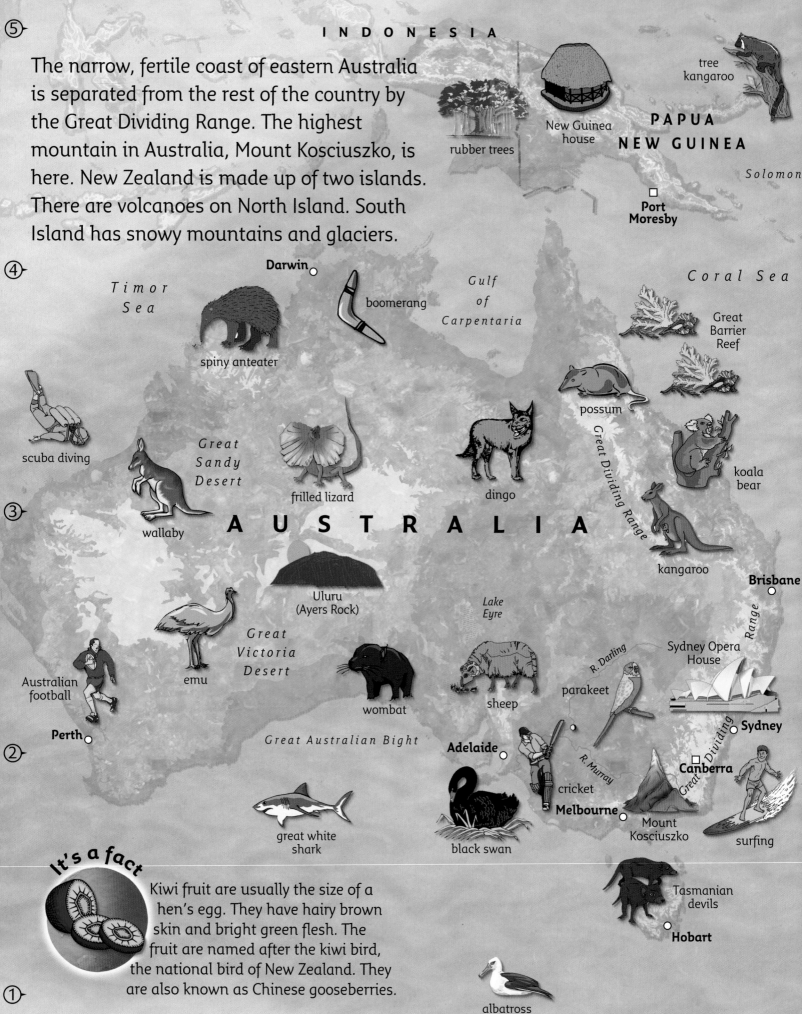

⑤

INDONESIA

The narrow, fertile coast of eastern Australia is separated from the rest of the country by the Great Dividing Range. The highest mountain in Australia, Mount Kosciuszko, is here. New Zealand is made up of two islands. There are volcanoes on North Island. South Island has snowy mountains and glaciers.

rubber trees

New Guinea house

tree kangaroo

PAPUA NEW GUINEA

Solomon

□ **Port Moresby**

④

Timor Sea

Darwin

spiny anteater

boomerang

Gulf of Carpentaria

Coral Sea

Great Barrier Reef

possum

scuba diving

Great Sandy Desert

frilled lizard

dingo

Great Dividing Range

koala bear

③

wallaby

A U S T R A L I A

kangaroo

Brisbane

Uluru (Ayers Rock)

Lake Eyre

Range

Australian football

emu

Great Victoria Desert

wombat

sheep

parakeet

Sydney Opera House

R. Darling

Perth

Great Australian Bight

Adelaide

cricket

R. Murray

Sydney

②

great white shark

black swan

Melbourne

Mount Kosciuszko

Great Dividing

Canberra

surfing

It's a fact

Kiwi fruit are usually the size of a hen's egg. They have hairy brown skin and bright green flesh. The fruit are named after the kiwi bird, the national bird of New Zealand. They are also known as Chinese gooseberries.

Tasmanian devils

Hobart

①

albatross

Ⓐ   Ⓑ   Ⓒ

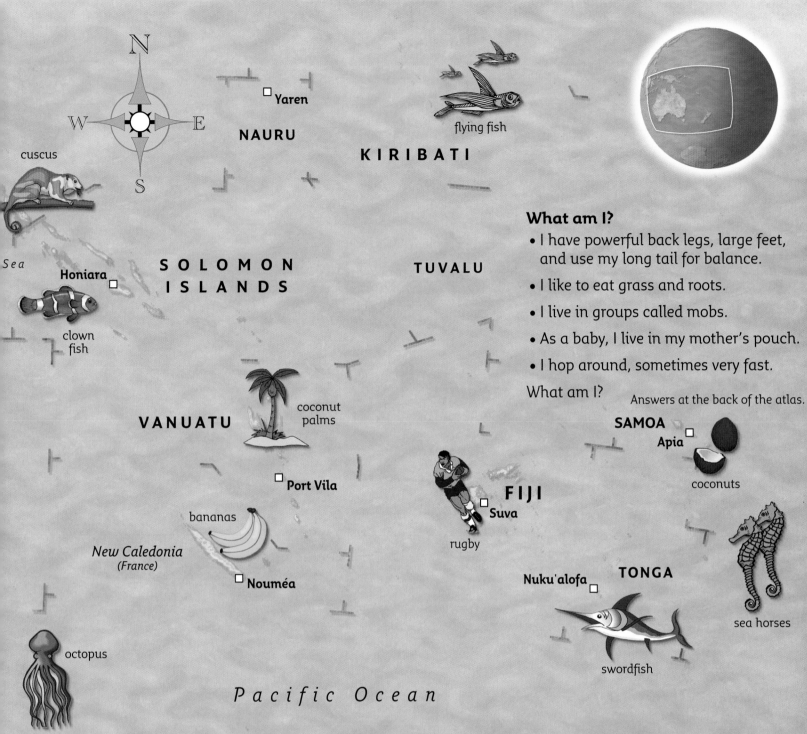

cuscus

NAURU
□ Yaren

KIRIBATI

flying fish

Sea

SOLOMON
ISLANDS

Honiara □

clown
fish

TUVALU

What am I?

• I have powerful back legs, large feet, and use my long tail for balance.

• I like to eat grass and roots.

• I live in groups called mobs.

• As a baby, I live in my mother's pouch.

• I hop around, sometimes very fast.

What am I?

Answers at the back of the atlas.

VANUATU

coconut
palms

SAMOA
Apia □

coconuts

□ Port Vila

bananas

New Caledonia
(France)

□ Nouméa

FIJI
□ Suva

rugby

Nuku'alofa □

TONGA

sea horses

swordfish

octopus

Pacific   Ocean

Try this!

There are many kinds of birds and sea creatures in this region. Look at the map and find

1 black bird
4 types of sea creature

Answers at the back of the atlas.

barracudas

kiwi

Auckland ○

rugby

volcanoes

kiwi
fruit

Wellington □

NEW
ZEALAND

Did you know?

• This region is on the opposite side of the world to Europe.

• It takes 3 days and 3 nights to cross Australia by train, from Perth to Sydney.

• On South Island, New Zealand, there are more sheep than people.

• There is natural hot steam underground on North Island. The steam is used to produce electricity.

• There are more than 850 native languages used in Papua New Guinea.

Tasman
Sea

sheep

takahe

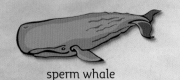

sperm whale

The Arctic Ocean

The Arctic Ocean is at the North Pole. Much of the sea is covered in ice all year round. It is the smallest and shallowest ocean in the world.

Try this!

Look at the map and find

1 type of air transport
1 type of water transport
1 type of land transport

Answers at the back of the atlas.

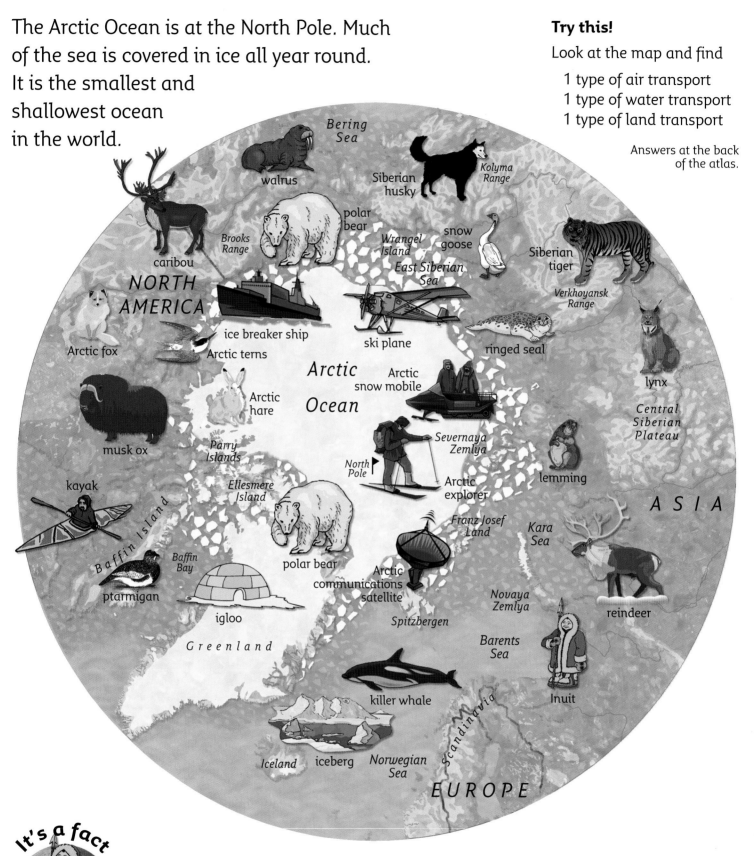

Bering Sea

walrus

Siberian husky

Kolyma Range

polar bear

snow goose

Wrangel Island

East Siberian Sea

Siberian tiger

caribou

Brooks Range

NORTH AMERICA

Verkhoyansk Range

Arctic fox

ice breaker ship

Arctic terns

ski plane

ringed seal

lynx

Arctic hare

Arctic Ocean

Arctic snow mobile

Central Siberian Plateau

musk ox

Parry Islands

North Pole

Severnaya Zemlya

lemming

kayak

Ellesmere Island

Arctic explorer

ASIA

Baffin Island

Baffin Bay

polar bear

Franz Josef Land

Kara Sea

ptarmigan

igloo

Arctic communications satellite

Novaya Zemlya

reindeer

Greenland

Spitzbergen

Barents Sea

Inuit

killer whale

Scandinavia

Iceland   iceberg   Norwegian Sea

EUROPE

It's a fact

The Inuit are a group of people native to the coasts of the Arctic Ocean. They have lived there for over 1000 years. Inuit are hunters and fishermen. Mostly they hunt caribou and seal. Inuit fish from boats called kayaks, a type of canoe. They travel across the snow and ice on sledges pulled by teams of dogs. Their language, Inukitut, uses symbols instead of letters.

Did you know?

- The permanent ice of the Arctic Ocean is about 4 metres (13 feet) thick.

- The Arctic is the least salty of all the oceans.

- It never rains in the Arctic Ocean – it only snows.

Antarctica

Antarctica is the area of thick ice surrounding the South Pole. It is the coldest, windiest and driest continent.

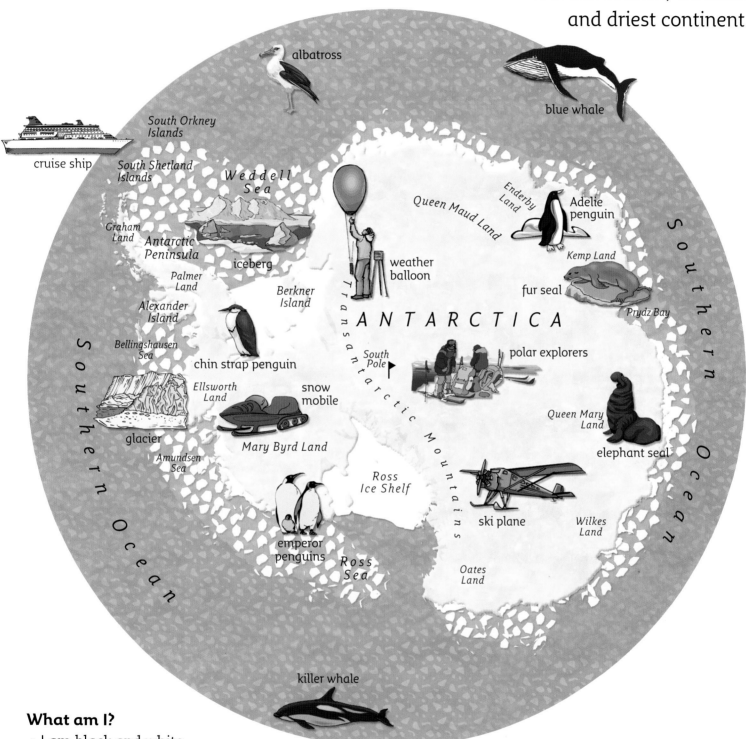

albatross

blue whale

cruise ship

South Orkney Islands

South Shetland Islands

Weddell Sea

Graham Land

Antarctic Peninsula

iceberg

Palmer Land

Berkner Island

Alexander Island

Bellingshausen Sea

chin strap penguin

Ellsworth Land

snow mobile

glacier

Mary Byrd Land

Amundsen Sea

emperor penguins

Ross Sea

Southern Ocean

Southern Ocean

Southern Ocean

Queen Maud Land

Enderby Land

Adelie penguin

Kemp Land

fur seal

Prydz Bay

ANTARCTICA

Transantarctic Mountains

South Pole

polar explorers

Queen Mary Land

elephant seal

Ross Ice Shelf

ski plane

Wilkes Land

Oates Land

weather balloon

killer whale

What am I?

- I am black and white.
- I eat fish and other sea life.
- I spend half my life on land and half in the sea.
- I am an excellent swimmer.
- On land I waddle on my feet, or slide on my tummy.
- I have wings but cannot fly.

What am I?

Answers at the back of the atlas.

Did you know?

- No one country owns Antarctica.
- No one lives permanently in Antarctica. Scientists visit to learn about the area.
- Many features on Antarctica are named after explorers.

Where have you been?

This world map shows some of the most visited countries in the world. You may have also visited some of these places. Perhaps you spent a holiday or visited friends and relations in these countries.

Look at the comments from children who have spent some time travelling in far away places. Would you agree with their comments or have you more interesting stories to tell?

Barcelona
Barcelona has lots of great shops and the weather is brilliant. It has lots of beaches.
Sophie 10 years

Greece
It's really hot and has lots of outdoor swimming pools and all the times I've been there there's been some really cute cats.
Vicki 10 years

Scotland
I really like the lochs, mountains and forests. The history is definitely the best.
Jake 10 years

CANADA

UNITED STATES OF AMERICA

BERMUDA

MEXICO

Australia
We built sand castles on the beach.
David 6 years

Spain
My favourite place is Salou in Spain because there is a huge theme park, Port Aventura.
Taylor 10 years

London
In London it is very cold in the winter. My Gran lives there. I love London.
Jasmin 10 years

Czech Republic
The Czech Republic is a beautiful place. I visit there with my Gran to see my cousins.
Isaac 10 years

Top 10 countries visited
1. France
2. Spain
3. United States of America
4. China
5. Italy
6. United Kingdom
7. Mexico
8. Germany
9. Turkey
10. Austria

Turkey
The food was nice, especially the lovely cherries from the market near Bodrum! We saw camels and I had a ride on one of them. The best thing was doing back flips on a bungee trampoline.
Charley 10 years

Slovakia
I really liked the snow and building a giant snowman, falling into the snow and skiing.
Marek 4 years

What do you think?

France

I was in France whilst they were in the final of the World Cup. I got to stay up late and make as much noise as I could without being heard.

Calum 10 years

Portugal

I like the swimming pools outside.

Cain 10 years

France

I used to live in France. I will always have this memory. One day it went snowy, sun, snow, sun etc....

Cameron 10 years

GERMANY

UNITED KINGDOM

CZECH REP.

IRELAND

SLOVAKIA

FRANCE

AUSTRIA

ITALY

PORTUGAL

SPAIN

GREECE

TURKEY

CHINA

INDIA

Scotland

The most exciting thing was when I was panning for gold at the Wanlockhead Lead Mine Museum and found some in the bottom of my pan.

Callum 8 years

MALAYSIA

KENYA

SOUTH AFRICA

AUSTRALIA

NEW ZEALAND

Florida

We went to Disneyworld to see Mickey Mouse. It was very hot.

Brad 7 years

Majorca

It is famous because it has a Pirate Show. Its main place is Palma.

Ross 10 years

Scotland

My favourite place is Loch Lomond.

Jordan 10 years

Scotland

I went to Millport. It was thunder and lightning. It struck a lamppost and it fell down on the road.

Antonio 10 years

Scotland

Edinburgh Dungeons has the most scary weirdest monsters in the world. I got the monster stuck in my dreams.

Brian 10 years

Disneyland Paris

Disneyland was great. It was sad when I had to leave.

Daniel 10 years

Spain

I liked Majorca because of the sun and the price of shopping. It was also really good because of the big beaches.

Kieran 10 years

Where have you been?

There are many reasons to travel to far away places. The symbols around this map show a selection of these. Names on the map tell us some of the best places to visit.

More interesting stories are also shown.

Sightseeing

North

America

Beach holiday

Eu

Med

Rocky Mountains

S a h

Winter sports

Caribbean Cruise
Sea

USA

I like Universal Studio because it has fantastic rides. I would give it a ten out of ten.

Sam 10 years

Bird watching

South

America

A
n
d
e
s

Desert Safari

Kenya

We were in a big car and saw elephants and lions. I liked the lions but they had big teeth. It was very dusty and hot.

Katie 7 years

USA

I used to live in Vermont. In winter it snows a lot and in the summer it is very hot.

Aidan 10 years

India

India is the greatest place ever.

Naomi 10 years

Exploring

A n t a

Malaysia

We went to the jungle and saw lots of animals in the trees. I was scared because the animals made lots of noise at night. It was hot but it rained every day.

Kim 8 years

Australia

I love Australia because of all the different animals on land and in the water and all of the lovely weather.

Robbie 10 years

Canary Islands

My favourite place is Tenerife because it's very comfortable...

Darren 10 years

Cadiz, Spain

My feet were almost burnt when I went on the beaches because the sand was so hot. Luckily the water cooled me down.

What do you think?

Turkey

It's really HOT!! I sleep walked into the hallway of our dormitory and I had nightmares about one of my Aunt's friend's cousins.

Sean 10 years

Scotland

Arran is an island off the southwest coast of Scotland. The funniest thing is when my friend catapults people across the bedroom with his feet. The best thing was when I got to ride a horse through a river on a pony trek.

Rona 10 years

South Africa

It was hot. We went on a boat and saw fish in the sea. I had a sore tummy in the boat.

Cameron 5 years

Greece

Rhodes in Greece is quiet with fantastic beaches.

Martha 10 years

Spain

My favourite city is Barcelona because it is very lively.

Megan 10 years

New Zealand

We made snowballs to throw at each other. But it was very cold.

Sophie 8 years

Canada

I love Canada because of the cool stuff to see and it is only 1 hour away from Disneyland.

Makeila 10 years

Ireland

My Great Granny lives in Ireland. It has great restaurants.

Molly 10 years

Barcelona

Barcelona has lots of great shops and the weather is brilliant. It has lots of beaches.

Sophie 10 years

USA

Florida is where I always go with my family. There are lots of things to do like rides and stuff.

Megan 10 years

Bermuda

Bermuda is always peaceful and quiet.

Callum 10 years

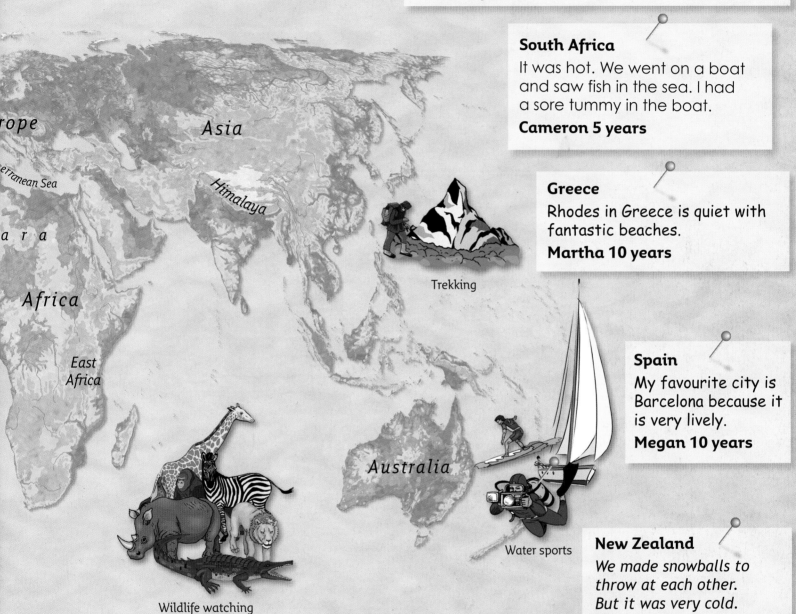

Trekking

Water sports

Wildlife watching

rope

Asia

Himalaya

terranean Sea

ara

Africa

East Africa

Australia

rctica

Countries of the World

Flag	COUNTRY, CONTINENT / Capital City / Population	Area square kilometres (square miles)
	AFGHANISTAN, ASIA / Kabul / 29 863 000	652 225 (251 825)
	ALBANIA, EUROPE / Tirana / 3 130 000	28 748 (11 100)
	ALGERIA, AFRICA / Algiers / 32 854 000	2 381 741 (919 595)
	ANGOLA, AFRICA / Luanda / 15 941 000	1 246 700 (481 353)
	ARGENTINA, SOUTH AMERICA / Buenos Aires / 38 747 000	2 766 889 (1 068 302)
	ARMENIA, ASIA / Yerevan / 3 016 000	29 800 (11 506)
	AUSTRALIA, OCEANIA / Canberra / 20 155 000	7 692 024 (2 969 907)
	AUSTRIA, EUROPE / Vienna / 8 189 000	83 855 (32 377)
	BAHRAIN, ASIA / Manama / 727 000	691 (267)
	BANGLADESH, ASIA / Dhaka / 141 822 000	143 998 (55 598)
	BELARUS, EUROPE / Minsk / 9 755 000	207 600 (80 155)
	BELGIUM, EUROPE / Brussels / 10 419 000	30 520 (11 784)
	BENIN, AFRICA / Porto Novo / 8 439 000	112 620 (43 483)
	BHUTAN, ASIA / Thimphu / 2 163 000	46 620 (18 000)
	BOLIVIA, SOUTH AMERICA / La Paz/Sucre / 9 182 000	1 098 581 (424 164)
	BOSNIA-HERZEGOVINA, EUROPE / Sarajevo / 3 907 000	51 130 (19 741)
	BOTSWANA, AFRICA / Gaborone / 1 765 000	581 370 (224 468)
	BRAZIL, SOUTH AMERICA / Brasília / 186 405 000	8 514 879 (3 287 613)
	BRUNEI, ASIA / Bandar Seri Begawan / 374 000	5 765 (2 226)
	BULGARIA, EUROPE / Sofia / 7 726 000	110 994 (42 855)
	BURKINA, AFRICA / Ouagadougou / 13 228 000	274 200 (105 869)
	BURUNDI, AFRICA / Bujumbura / 7 548 000	27 835 (10 747)
	CAMBODIA, ASIA / Phnom Penh / 14 071 000	181 035 (69 884)
	CAMEROON, AFRICA / Yaoundé / 16 322 000	475 442 (183 569)
	CANADA, NORTH AMERICA / Ottawa / 32 268 000	9 984 670 (3 855 103)
	CENTRAL AFRICAN REPUBLIC, AFRICA / Bangui / 4 038 000	622 436 (240 324)
	CHAD, AFRICA / Ndjamena / 9 749 000	1 284 000 (495 755)
	CHILE, SOUTH AMERICA / Santiago / 16 295 000	756 945 (292 258)
	CHINA, ASIA / Beijing / 1 323 345 000	9 584 492 (3 700 593)
	COLOMBIA, SOUTH AMERICA / Bogotá / 45 600 000	1 141 748 (440 831)
	CONGO, AFRICA / Brazzaville / 3 999 000	342 000 (132 047)
	CONGO, DEMOCRATIC REPUBLIC OF THE AFRICA / Kinshasa / 57 549 000	2 345 410 (905 568)
	COSTA RICA, NORTH AMERICA / San José / 4 327 000	51 100 (19 730)
	CÔTE D'IVOIRE, AFRICA / Yamoussoukro / 18 154 000	322 463 (124 504)
	CROATIA, EUROPE / Zagreb / 4 551 000	56 538 (21 829)
	CUBA, NORTH AMERICA / Havana / 11 269 000	110 860 (42 803)
	CYPRUS, ASIA / Nicosia / 835 000	9 251 (3 572)
	CZECH REPUBLIC, EUROPE / Prague / 10 220 000	78 864 (30 450)
	DENMARK, EUROPE / Copenhagen / 5 431 000	43 075 (16 631)

DJIBOUTI, AFRICA
🏙 Djibouti
👥 793 000
✉ 23 200
(8 958)

DOMINICAN REPUBLIC, NORTH AMERICA
🏙 Santo Domingo
👥 8 895 000
✉ 48 442
(18 704)

EAST TIMOR, ASIA
🏙 Dili
👥 947 000
✉ 14 874
(5 743)

ECUADOR, SOUTH AMERICA
🏙 Quito
👥 13 228 000
✉ 272 045
(105 037)

EGYPT, AFRICA
🏙 Cairo
👥 74 033 000
✉ 1 000 250
(386 199)

EL SALVADOR, NORTH AMERICA
🏙 San Salvador
👥 6 881 000
✉ 21 041
(8 124)

EQUATORIAL GUINEA, AFRICA
🏙 Malabo
👥 504 000
✉ 28 051
(10 831)

ERITREA, AFRICA
🏙 Asmara
👥 4 401 000
✉ 117 400
(45 328)

ESTONIA, EUROPE
🏙 Tallinn
👥 1 330 000
✉ 45 200
(17 452)

ETHIOPIA, AFRICA
🏙 Addis Ababa
👥 77 431 000
✉ 1 133 880
(437 794)

FINLAND, EUROPE
🏙 Helsinki
👥 5 249 000
✉ 338 145
(130 559)

FRANCE, EUROPE
🏙 Paris
👥 60 496 000
✉ 543 965
(210 026)

GABON, AFRICA
🏙 Libreville
👥 1 384 000
✉ 267 667
(103 347)

GEORGIA, ASIA
🏙 T'bilisi
👥 4 474 000
✉ 69 700
(26 911)

GERMANY, EUROPE
🏙 Berlin
👥 82 689 000
✉ 357 022
(137 849)

GHANA, AFRICA
🏙 Accra
👥 22 113 000
✉ 238 537
(92 100)

GREECE, EUROPE
🏙 Athens
👥 11 120 000
✉ 131 957
(50 949)

GUATEMALA, NORTH AMERICA
🏙 Guatemala City
👥 12 599 000
✉ 108 890
(42 043)

GUINEA, AFRICA
🏙 Conakry
👥 6 402 000
✉ 245 857
(94 926)

GUINEA-BISSAU, AFRICA
🏙 Bissau
👥 1 586 000
✉ 36 125
(13 948)

GUYANA, SOUTH AMERICA
🏙 Georgetown
👥 751 000
✉ 214 969
(83 000)

HAITI, NORTH AMERICA
🏙 Port-au-Prince
👥 8 528 000
✉ 27 750
(10 714)

HONDURAS, NORTH AMERICA
🏙 Tegucigalpa
👥 7 205 000
✉ 112 088
(43 277)

HUNGARY, EUROPE
🏙 Budapest
👥 10 098 000
✉ 93 030
(35 919)

ICELAND, EUROPE
🏙 Reykjavik
👥 295 000
✉ 102 820
(39 699)

INDIA, ASIA
🏙 New Delhi
👥 1 103 371 000
✉ 3 064 898
(1 183 364)

INDONESIA, ASIA
🏙 Jakarta
👥 222 781 000
✉ 1 919 445
(741 102)

IRAN, ASIA
🏙 Tehran
👥 69 515 000
✉ 1 648 000
(636 296)

IRAQ, ASIA
🏙 Baghdad
👥 28 807 000
✉ 438 317
(169 235)

IRELAND EUROPE
🏙 Dublin
👥 4 148 000
✉ 70 282
(27 136)

ISRAEL, ASIA
🏙 Jerusalem
👥 6 725 000
✉ 20 770
(8 019)

ITALY, EUROPE
🏙 Rome
👥 58 093 000
✉ 301 245
(116 311)

JAMAICA, NORTH AMERICA
🏙 Kingston
👥 2 651 000
✉ 10 991
(4 244)

JAPAN, ASIA
🏙 Tokyo
👥 128 085 000
✉ 377 727
(145 841)

JORDAN, ASIA
🏙 Amman
👥 5 703 000
✉ 89 206
(34 443)

KAZAKHSTAN, ASIA
🏙 Astana
👥 14 825 000
✉ 2 717 300
(1 049 155)

KENYA, AFRICA
🏙 Nairobi
👥 34 256 000
✉ 582 646
(224 961)

KUWAIT, ASIA
🏙 Kuwait
👥 2 687 000
✉ 17 818
(6 880)

KYRGYZSTAN, ASIA
🏙 Bishkek
👥 5 264 000
✉ 198 500
(76 641)

LAOS, ASIA
🏙 Vientiane
👥 5 924 000
✉ 236 800
(91 429)

Countries of the World

LATVIA, EUROPE
Riga
2 307 000
63 700
(24 595)

LEBANON, ASIA
Beirut
3 577 000
10 452
(4 036)

LESOTHO, AFRICA
Maseru
1 795 000
30 355
(11 720)

LIBERIA, AFRICA
Monrovia
3 283 000
111 369
(43 000)

LIBYA, AFRICA
Tripoli
5 853 000
1 759 540
(679 362)

LITHUANIA, EUROPE
Vilnius
3 431 000
65 200
(25 174)

LUXEMBOURG, EUROPE
Luxembourg
465 000
2 586
(998)

MACEDONIA, EUROPE
Skopje
2 034 000
25 713
(9 928)

MADAGASCAR, AFRICA
Antananarivo
18 606 000
587 041
(226 658)

MALAWI, AFRICA
Lilongwe
12 884 000
118 484
(45 747)

MALAYSIA, ASIA
Kuala Lumpur/Putrajaya
25 347 000
332 965
(128 559)

MALI, AFRICA
Bamako
13 518 000
1 240 140
(478 821)

MAURITANIA, AFRICA
Nouakchott
3 069 000
1 030 700
(397 955)

MEXICO, NORTH AMERICA
Mexico City
107 029 000
1 972 545
(761 604)

MONGOLIA, ASIA
Ulan Bator
2 646 000
1 565 000
(604 250)

MONTENEGRO, EUROPE
Podgorica
620 000
13 812
(5333)

MOROCCO, AFRICA
Rabat
31 478 000
446 550
(172 414)

MOZAMBIQUE, AFRICA
Maputo
19 792 000
799 380
(308 642)

MYANMAR (BURMA), ASIA
Naypyidaw/Yangon
50 519 000
676 577
(261 228)

NAMIBIA, AFRICA
Windhoek
2 031 000
824 292
(318 261)

NEPAL, ASIA
Kathmandu
27 133 000
147 181
(56 827)

NETHERLANDS, EUROPE
Amsterdam/The Hague
16 299 000
41 526
(16 033)

NEW ZEALAND, OCEANIA
Wellington
4 028 000
270 534
(104 454)

NICARAGUA, NORTH AMERICA
Managua
5 487 000
130 000
(50 193)

NIGER, AFRICA
Niamey
13 957 000
1 267 000
(489 191)

NIGERIA, AFRICA
Abuja
131 530 000
923 768
(356 669)

NORTH KOREA, ASIA
Pyongyang
22 488 000
120 538
(46 540)

NORWAY, EUROPE
Oslo
4 620 000
323 878
(125 050)

OMAN, ASIA
Muscat
2 567 000
309 500
(119 499)

PAKISTAN, ASIA
Islamabad
157 935 000
803 940
(310 403)

PANAMA, NORTH AMERICA
Panama City
3 232 000
77 082
(29 762)

PAPUA NEW GUINEA, OCEANIA
Port Moresby
5 887 000
462 840
(178 704)

PARAGUAY, SOUTH AMERICA
Asunción
6 158 000
406 752
(157 048)

PERU, SOUTH AMERICA
Lima
27 968 000
1 285 216
(496 225)

PHILIPPINES, ASIA
Manila
83 054 000
300 000
(115 831)

POLAND, EUROPE
Warsaw
38 530 000
312 683
(120 728)

PORTUGAL, EUROPE
Lisbon
10 495 000
88 940
(34 340)

QATAR, ASIA
Doha
813 000
11 437
(4 416)

ROMANIA, EUROPE
Bucharest
21 711 000
237 500
(91 699)

RUSSIAN FEDERATION, EUROPE/ASIA
Moscow
143 202 000
17 075 400
(6 592 849)

SAUDI ARABIA, ASIA
Riyadh
24 573 000
2 200 000
(849 425)

SENEGAL, AFRICA
Dakar
11 658 000
196 720
(75 954)

SERBIA, EUROPE
Belgrade
9 379 000
88 361
(34 116)

SIERRA LEONE, AFRICA
Freetown
5 525 000
71 740
(27 699)

SINGAPORE, ASIA
Singapore
4 326 000
639
(247)

SLOVAKIA, EUROPE
Bratislava
5 401 000
49 035
(18 933)

SLOVENIA, EUROPE
Ljubljana
1 967 000
20 251
(7 819)

SOMALIA, AFRICA
Mogadishu
8 228 000
637 657
(246 201)

SOUTH AFRICA, REPUBLIC OF AFRICA
Pretoria/Cape Town
47 432 000
1 219 090
(470 693)

SOUTH KOREA, ASIA
Seoul
47 817 000
99 274
(38 330)

SPAIN, EUROPE
Madrid
43 064 000
504 782
(194 897)

SRI LANKA, ASIA
Sri Jayewardenepura Kotte
20 743 000
65 610
(25 332)

SUDAN, AFRICA
Khartoum
36 233 000
2 505 813
(967 500)

SURINAME, SOUTH AMERICA
Paramaribo
449 000
163 820
(63 251)

SWAZILAND, AFRICA
Mbabane
1 032 000
17 364
(6 704)

SWEDEN, EUROPE
Stockholm
9 041 000
449 964
(173 732)

SWITZERLAND, EUROPE
Bern
7 252 000
41 293
(15 943)

SYRIA, ASIA
Damascus
19 043 000
185 180
(71 498)

TAIWAN, ASIA
T'aipei
22 858 000
36 179
(13 969)

TAJIKISTAN, ASIA
Dushanbe
6 507 000
143 100
(55 251)

TANZANIA, AFRICA
Dodoma
38 329 000
945 087
(364 900)

THAILAND, ASIA
Bangkok
64 233 000
513 115
(198 115)

THE GAMBIA, AFRICA
Banjul
1 517 000
11 295
(4 361)

TOGO, AFRICA
Lomé
6 145 000
56 785
(21 925)

TRINIDAD AND TOBAGO, NORTH AMERICA
Port of Spain
1 305 000
5 130
(1 981)

TUNISIA, AFRICA
Tunis
10 102 000
164 150
(63 379)

TURKEY, ASIA/EUROPE
Ankara
73 193 000
779 452
(300 948)

TURKMENISTAN, ASIA
Ashgabat
4 833 000
488 100
(188 456)

UGANDA, AFRICA
Kampala
28 816 000
241 038
(93 065)

UKRAINE, EUROPE
Kiev
46 481 000
603 700
(233 090)

UNITED ARAB EMIRATES, ASIA
Abu Dhabi
4 496 000
77 700
(30 000)

UNITED KINGDOM, EUROPE
London
59 668 000
243 609
(94 058)

UNITED STATES OF AMERICA, NORTH AMERICA
Washington
298 213 000
9 826 635
(3 794 085)

URUGUAY, SOUTH AMERICA
Montevideo
3 463 000
176 215
(68 037)

UZBEKISTAN, ASIA
Tashkent
26 593 000
447 400
(172 742)

VENEZUELA, SOUTH AMERICA
Caracas
26 749 000
912 050
(352 144)

VIETNAM, ASIA
Hanoi
84 238 000
329 565
(127 246)

YEMEN, ASIA
San'a
20 975 000
527 968
(203 850)

ZAMBIA, AFRICA
Lusaka
11 668 000
752 614
(290 586)

ZIMBABWE, AFRICA
Harare
13 010 000
390 759
(150 873)

Games and Quizzes

Name the continents
Match the numbers on the map to the continent names listed.

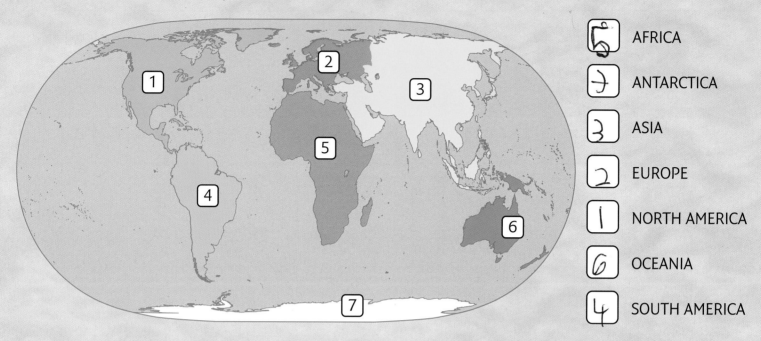

5	AFRICA
7	ANTARCTICA
3	ASIA
2	EUROPE
1	NORTH AMERICA
6	OCEANIA
4	SOUTH AMERICA

Name the countries
Match the shapes to the country names listed.

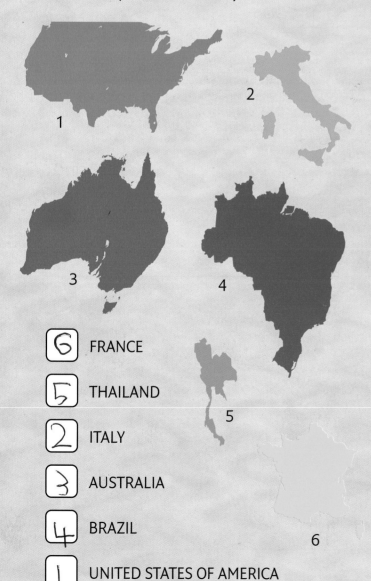

1

2

3

4

5

6

6	FRANCE
5	THAILAND
2	ITALY
3	AUSTRALIA
4	BRAZIL
1	UNITED STATES OF AMERICA

Search for cities
The 12 capital cities listed below are hidden in this grid. See how many you can find.

A	O	W	E	L	L	I	N	G	T	O	N
B	P	X	Z	P	O	J	X	Z	Q	J	O
W	A	S	H	I	N	G	T	O	N	V	T
X	R	K	Y	Y	D	W	V	J	F	X	T
C	I	K	P	F	O	X	Z	Q	J	F	A
A	S	Z	B	A	N	G	K	O	K	X	W
N	J	V	Q	Z	X	X	C	H	Z	Y	A
B	R	A	S	I	L	I	A	W	X	T	V
E	W	H	G	M	X	Z	I	Z	F	U	X
R	O	M	E	X	Q	V	R	J	Q	N	F
R	V	W	T	O	K	Y	O	V	W	I	Q
A	Q	W	H	G	M	X	T	J	V	S	Q

~~LONDON~~   ~~WELLINGTON~~   CAIRO
~~PARIS~~   TOKYO   TUNIS
ROME   BANGKOK   OTTAWA
CANBERRA   BRASILIA   ~~WASHINGTON~~

Quiz 1
1. What is the largest country in the world?

   Russia

2. What is the capital of France?

   Paris

3. What colour is the flag of Libya?

   green

56

Colour match

All these symbols have a colour in part of their name. Find their correct name by matching a colour with one of the other words.

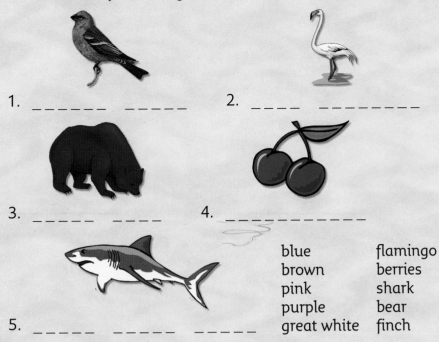

1. _ _ _ _ _ _ _ _ _ _ _

2. _ _ _ _ _ _ _ _ _ _ _ _

3. _ _ _ _ _ _ _ _ _

4. _ _ _ _ _ _ _ _ _ _ _

5. _ _ _ _ _ _ _ _ _ _ _ _ _ _ _

blue   flamingo
brown   berries
pink   shark
purple   bear
great white finch

Unscramble the countries

Rearrange the letters in the boxes to find the names of 6 countries.

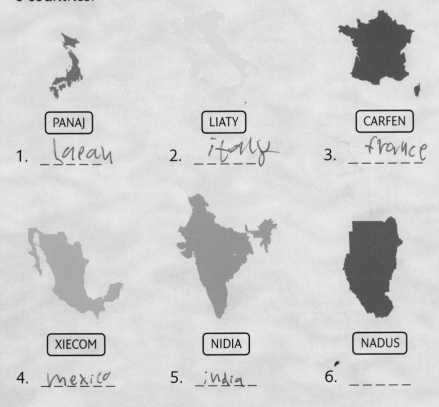

| PANAJ |
1. _japan_

| LIATY |
2. _italy_

| CARFEN |
3. _france_

| XIECOM |
4. _mexico_

| NIDIA |
5. _india_

| NADUS |
6. _ _ _ _ _

Quiz 2

1. What is the world's longest river?

2. How many colours are on the flag of Italy?

   3

3. What kind of bears are found in Arctic regions?

   a- polar

Whose flag is this?

There are 16 country flags and 16 country names shown below. Try to match up the country names to their flag. Add the correct flag number to the box beside each country name.

| 9 | CHINA | 12 | JAPAN |

| 1 | CANADA | 3 | GREECE |

| 5 | PAKISTAN | 13 | NEPAL |

| 7 | BRAZIL | 14 | SOMALIA |

| 16 | CHILE | 6 | SWEDEN |

| 2 | AUSTRALIA | 8 | KENYA |

| 11 | NEW ZEALAND |

| 10 | UNITED KINGDOM |

| 15 | REPUBLIC OF SOUTH AFRICA |

| 4 | UNITED STATES OF AMERICA |

Answers on page 64.

Games and Quizzes

Name the oceans

Match the numbers on the map to the ocean names listed.

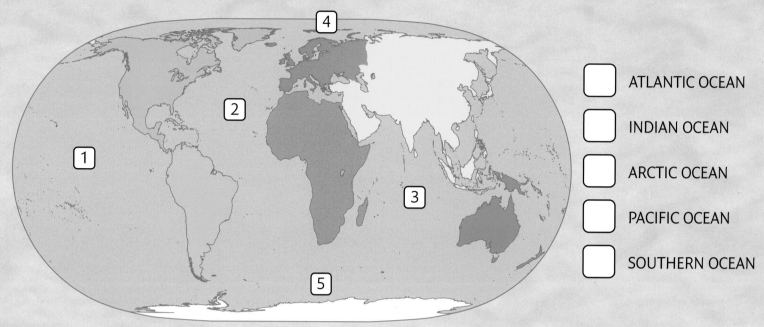

- [ ] ATLANTIC OCEAN
- [ ] INDIAN OCEAN
- [ ] ARCTIC OCEAN
- [ ] PACIFIC OCEAN
- [ ] SOUTHERN OCEAN

Name the symbol

Choose a suitable caption for each symbol from the names in the panel on the right.
Only one caption will match each symbol.

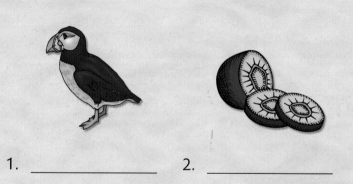

1. _____   2. _____

Puffin	Kiwi fruit	Owl
	Bobcat	Polar bear
Grapes	Taj Mahal	
Stonehenge	Hockey	Apple
Walrus	Banana	Cricket
Oil platform	Shamrock	
	Sydney Opera House	

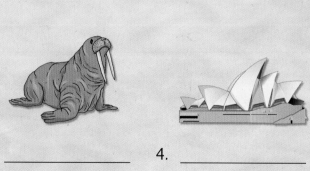

3. _____   4. _____

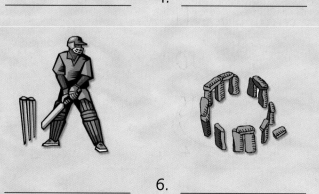

5. _____   6. _____

Quiz 3

1. What is the capital of Argentina?

2. How many blue stripes appear on the flag of Honduras?

3. In which country would you watch this sport?

Symbol Match

In which country would you expect to see these?
Add the correct symbol number to the box beside each country name.

 1. Tower Bridge

 2. Croissants

 3. Liberty Bell

 4. Taj Mahal

 5. Kangaroo

6. Zulu house

3	UNITED STATES OF AMERICA		2	FRANCE
1	UNITED KINGDOM		6 ⟩ 2	SWAZILAND
4	INDIA		5	AUSTRALIA

Which continent are you in?

Look at the groups of flags below.
Which continent would you be in if these flags were shown?

1.

2.

3.

4.

5.

6.

4	ASIA	5	OCEANIA
1	EUROPE	3	NORTH AMERICA
6	SOUTH AMERICA	2	AFRICA

Search for countries

The 10 countries listed below are hidden in this grid.
See how many you can find.

A	R	G	E	N	T	I	N	A	F	K	Y
N	V	G	F	Y	N	E	Z	U	Z	B	V
C	Y	D	Q	C	G	G	G	S	X	Q	J
H	U	N	G	A	R	Y	B	T	G	B	J
I	L	A	F	N	G	P	H	R	B	O	Q
N	N	L	Z	A	S	T	V	A	P	T	X
A	G	O	X	D	T	V	F	L	H	S	F
H	P	O	L	A	N	D	Z	I	H	W	F
H	Y	X	Q	Q	V	Z	X	A	Z	A	O
M	E	X	I	C	O	G	G	V	G	N	Q
Q	Z	J	B	Y	F	F	B	X	B	A	J
N	I	G	E	R	I	A	B	J	Q	K	P

ARGENTINA
AUSTRALIA
BOTSWANA
CANADA
CHINA
EGYPT
HUNGARY
MEXICO
NIGERIA
POLAND

Quiz 4

1. What is the world's highest mountain?

2. What is the capital of China?

3. In which country would you find these animals?

Answers on page 64.

Index

This index lists all the important place names shown on the maps. The grid code numbers and letters help you to find the correct position of the name on each map.

Answers

	Try this!		**What am I?**

2-3   GREENLAND

4-5
1. Canadian goose, Arctic tern, snowy owl, snow goose, ptarmigan
2. Newfoundland, husky
3. polar bear, musk ox, Arctic fox, wolf, brown bear, bobcat, caribou, moose, beaver, Arctic hare

A maple leaf

6-7
1. blueberries, grapes, oranges, apples
2. hotdog, hamburger, muffin
3. peanut

A hot dog

8-9
1. tropical fish, sea horse, great white shark, elephant seal, monk seal, turtle
2. parrot, toucan

A cactus

10-11 1. Colombia, Chile   2. Bogota, Brasilia

12-13 1. emerald, diamond   2. anaconda   A condor

14-15
1. mackerel, sardine
2. polo, skiing, football, motor racing

A killer whale

16-17 MADAGASCAR

18-19
1. camel, gerbil, baboon
2. scorpion, tortoise
3. hoopoe, hornbill bird, bee eater bird, secretary bird

A camel

20-21 1. grapes, oranges   2. cloves   A sand dune

22-23
1. Two. Germany and Belgium
2. Greece   3. Norway

24-25
1. football, cricket, rugby
2. yachting, windsurfing
3. curling, skiing

A shamrock

26-27
1. Gouda   2. dairy cows, pigs, sheep
3. croissant

An owl

28-29   Spaghetti

30-31 Sri Lanka

32-33
1. reindeer, polar bear, Siberian tiger, Siberian husky, Siberian stag, brown bear, lynx, Caspian seal, lemming
2. eider duck, snow goose, Ural owl

A brown bear

34-35
1. Arabian camel, Arabian fox, Arabian horse
2. Mosque   3. cricket

A flamingo

36-37
1. tiger, snow leopard, Asiatic lion
2. peacock, parakeet   3. Indian porcupine

An octopus

38-39
1. Giant panda
2. karate, sumo wrestling, skiing

A terracotta soldier

40-41 1. surfing and scuba diving   A Komodo dragon

42-43   FIJI   AUSTRALIA   NAURU

44-45
1. black swan
2. sea horses, sperm whale, barracuda, flying fish, clown fish, great white shark, swordfish, octopus

A kangaroo

46
1. ski plane   2. kayak
3. snowmobile

47   A penguin

Answers

56-57   Games and quizzes

Name the continents
1. North America   2. Europe
3. Asia   4. South America
5. Africa   6. Oceania
7. Antarctica

Name the countries
1. United States of America
2. Italy   3. Australia
4. Brazil   5. Thailand
6. France

Search for cities

A	O	W	E	L	L	I	N	G	T	O	N
B	P	X	Z	P	O	J	X	Z	Q	J	O
W	A	S	H	I	N	G	T	O	N	V	T
X	R	K	Y	Y	D	W	V	J	F	X	T
C	I	K	P	F	O	X	Z	Q	J	F	A
A	S	Z	B	A	N	G	K	O	K	X	W
N	J	V	Q	Z	X	X	C	H	Z	Y	A
B	R	A	S	I	L	I	A	W	X	T	V
E	W	H	G	M	X	Z	I	Z	F	U	X
R	O	M	E	X	Q	V	R	J	Q	N	F
R	V	W	T	O	K	Y	O	V	W	I	Q
A	Q	W	H	G	M	X	T	J	V	S	Q

Quiz 1
1. Russian Federation   2. Paris
3. Green

Colour match
1. purple finch   2. pink flamingo
3. brown bear   4. blueberries
5. great white shark

Unscramble the countries
1. Japan   2. Italy
3. France   4. Mexico
5. India   6. Sudan

Quiz 2
1. River Nile   2. 3 (green, white and red)
3. Polar bears

Whose flag is this?
1. Canada   2. Australia
3. Greece   4. United States of America
5. Pakistan   6. Sweden
7. Brazil   8. Kenya
9. China   10. United Kingdom
11. New Zealand   12. Japan
13. Nepal   14. Chile
15. Republic of South Africa
16. Somalia

58-59   Games and quizzes

Name the oceans
1. Pacific Ocean   2. Atlantic Ocean
3. Indian Ocean   4. Arctic Ocean
5. Southern Ocean

Name the symbol
1. Puffin   2. Kiwi fruit
3. Walrus   4. Sydney Opera House
5. Cricket   6. Stonehenge

Quiz 3
1. Buenos Aires   2. 2
3. Japan

Symbol match
1. United Kingdom   2. France
3. United States of America
4. India   5. Australia
6. Swaziland

Which continent are you in?
1. Europe   2. Africa
3. North America   4. Asia
5. Oceania   6. South America

Search for countries

A	R	G	E	N	T	I	N	A	F	K	Y
N	V	G	F	Y	N	E	Z	U	Z	B	V
C	Y	D	Q	C	G	G	G	S	X	Q	J
H	U	N	G	A	R	Y	B	T	G	B	J
I	L	A	F	N	G	P	H	R	B	O	Q
N	N	L	Z	A	S	T	V	A	P	T	X
A	G	O	X	D	T	V	F	L	H	S	F
H	P	O	L	A	N	D	Z	I	H	W	F
H	Y	X	Q	Q	V	Z	X	A	Z	A	O
M	E	X	I	C	O	G	G	V	G	N	Q
Q	Z	J	B	Y	F	F	B	X	B	A	J
N	I	G	E	R	I	A	B	J	Q	K	P

Quiz 4
1. Mount Everest   2. Beijing
3. Australia